FRONTLINES

frontlines

FINDING MY VOICE ON AN
AMERICAN COLLEGE CAMPUS

ISABEL BROWN

HOUNDSTOOTH
PRESS

FRONTLINES
Finding My Voice on an American College Campus

ISBN 978-1-5445-1931-9 *Hardcover*
     978-1-5445-1930-2 *Paperback*
     978-1-5445-1929-6 *Ebook*

For Kelli and Rob, my parents, who always taught me that my voice is my most powerful tool to effectuate change—and that I'm never too young to start using it.

CONTENTS

DISCLAIMER

When necessary, names and identifying characteristics of individuals and places have been changed to protect privacy. Some events, places, and conversations have been recalled from memory, and some conversations have been recreated and/or supplemented. The chronology of some events has been compressed.

INTRODUCTION

I'm not supposed to be writing this book.

College alumni are supposed to feel nothing but pride for their alma maters, sporting spirit T-shirts on Saturdays, and flying their school flags on their front porches. I'm supposed to look back on my college years with nothing but fond memories, overjoyed by the four years of fun I was lucky enough to experience. I'm supposed to fill countless photo albums with smiling faces recounting memories from football games or nights out in town. I'm supposed to do everything in my power to write a big check to my alumni association every year, knowing it will help shape the experiences of happy, excited, new students.

I'm not supposed to expose the parts of college they don't want you to discover. I'm not supposed to tell the whole truth.

Of course, I did enjoy so much of my college experience. I played board games with the other students in my freshman dorm, laughing and telling stories. I drank way too many milkshakes in my dining hall (guilty) and met up with friends in the student center for coffee. I studied hard and deeply loved what I was learning (for the most part—not looking at you, Organic Chemistry). I went to parties, cheered at football games, and served in student government. I was, and still am, so deeply proud to be a Colorado State University (CSU) Ram.

But unlike many college students, I walked around campus with a heavy load—not just a backpack full of my science textbooks, but with the untold, cumbersome experience of being a conservative warrior in a world of leftist indoctrination. I endured situations no ordinary college student should have to face, simply because I had decided it was time for true intellectual diversity to exist at my university. I wanted to start a conversation about our differences of opinion—so why did that make me the number one target on my college campus?

Many of these stories have only been shared with my family and close friends. I will share with you the college experience that kept me up at night, the trials I chose to push through, and the hurt and isolation that surrounded my heart for months. I don't tell you these stories to play the victim. As you'll see, I've never felt victimized by these circumstances at all.

Rather, I tell you my story because it is *not* unique. The reality of the backlash I faced as a vocal conservative student activist is the norm for thousands of young Americans like me each and every day on American college campuses. We lose friendships and receive failing grades on assignments simply due to sharing our values, which may even jeopardize our personal safety. Knowing this is our reality, we courageously continue fighting for a conservative presence on our college campuses. We refuse to let American ideals be replaced by socialism. We refuse to let the Left win the culture war for the future of America.

If you are a bold conservative voice on your campus, thinking about sharing your unique perspective with your community or looking for guidance on the first step of your conservative journey, this book is for you. Gen Z is the most conservative generation our country has seen since World War II (according to several national polls), and we are inspiring one another to carry the torch of freedom forward.[1] At Turning Point USA, America's largest and fastest-growing conservative youth organization, we like to say that Gen Z is Gen Free. I am hopeful that by reading my story, you'll be energized to join us in the fight for America's culture.

If you are familiar with the world of conservative politics today, you've seen many faces of young political leaders often discussing the insanity occurring at our nation's universities. From Charlie Kirk to Candace Owens, and many more, these young politicos are drawing much-needed attention to how unreal the alternate reality of a college campus is. Most of these leaders and exceptional communicators have one thing in common: they are *not* current college students. You'll often hear these individuals and many more discussing the latest protest designed to block them or another conservative speaker from coming to campus.

However, the stories of ordinary, everyday students are

---

1   Ashley Stahl, "Why Democrats Should Be Losing Sleep Over Generation Z," *Forbes*, August 11, 2017, https://www.forbes.com/sites/ashleystahl/2017/08/11/why-democrats-should-be-losing-sleep-over-generation-z/?sh=789549f17878.

rarely published or shared with a large audience—the stories of a science professor exclaiming that gender is a social construct in the classroom, of administrators setting quotas on faculty positions dedicated to diversity, or of student fee dollars funding annual university-sponsored speakers like Bernie Sanders while denying equal time for conservative speakers.

It's time a conversation about our nation's college campuses is brought to light.

That's where I come in.

I recently concluded my journey as a graduate student—for now, anyway—at Georgetown University, having pursued a master's degree in Biomedical Sciences Policy and Advocacy. While my experience at Georgetown was academically and personally fulfilling and (mostly) free from indoctrination, my undergraduate premed experience at CSU was dramatically different. At CSU, I studied Biomedical Sciences and Spanish Language and began college with the intention of attending medical school after graduation. While I always had a personal interest in understanding current political events, I had no desire to work in politics before starting college. In fact, I was fairly uninvolved politically.

That all changed, however, about halfway through my college experience, when I began living the reality of leftist indoctrination on my campus every day. It was like a siren in my ear, drowning out my focused study of anatomy, chemistry, physiology, and genetics. It was at this point I knew if I did not speak up for conservative values on my campus, it was likely no one else would. This realization took me on an unexpected path toward political activism with Turning Point USA, internships in the US Senate and the White House for the Trump Administration, and pursuing a career in media and politics after graduation.

My campus story will share with you what happens behind the scenes at our nation's colleges—not just for a few hours when a famous conservative speaker or social media influencer comes to campus—but what was on my exams, spoken by my professors, promoted by my student government, and paid for by my student fees. It's a perspective that has yet to be fully shared, but one that many of us in Gen Z experience daily in dorms, dining halls, and classrooms. It's a story that must be told to preserve our American identity.

In the fall of 2018, mainstream media outlets began reporting on a comically absurd story from CSU about how the phrase "long time no see" had been officially deemed by university administrators and student government officials as "derogatory to those of Asian descent."[2] After sharing the news on my social media, I was contacted by a number of friends and family members jovially stating, "This must be a joke!" Surely, a university wouldn't go so far as to deem nearly *every* trivial phrase as offensive to some target population or another—this would yield silence from every student on campus.

As a senior in college at this point, having endured many such absurdities, I knew this was no laughing matter. Every word

---

2   Dave Urbanski, "'Long time, no see' reportedly deemed offensive at
     college. Why? It's derogatory toward Asians," *The Blaze*, last modified
     November 7, 2018, https://www.theblaze.com/news/2018/11/07/
     long-time-no-see-reportedly-deemed-offensive-at-college-why-its-derogatory-toward-asians.

written about the declaration rang of truth. Rather, this was the perfect illustration of my collegiate experience. Again, I will forever be "proud to be a CSU Ram," but throughout my four years as a college student, the political-correctness police had irreversibly altered nearly every aspect of the university setting, inside the classroom and out. I had gained substantial knowledge and academic understanding but collected significantly more baffling experiences and memories far removed from reality or even the substance of my curriculum. From being disciplined at my on-campus job after uttering the words "you guys" to being forced to state God was not the creator of the universe on a biology exam, most of these experiences are nearly impossible for most Americans to believe.

I believe that many individuals serving in the faculty and administration at my undergraduate university and other colleges across the nation do have the right intentions, particularly those in the hard sciences and hands-on programs, such as agriculture and mechanics. Many people are still fighting for education to provide the strongest learning institutions possible, but the reality is that most people running our nation's institutions of higher education are, intentionally or not, propagating a leftist machine that will only continue to degrade the exceptional educational standards we once had in America. This is especially true for "career academics," those who have never spent significant time in their adult lives away from a college campus and who later earn administrative positions at universities. That's why it's oh-so-important to have a massive contingent of faculty at nearly every institution in America dedicated to implementing "diversity initiatives" and changing the curriculum of our students' classes to fulfill the leftist agenda.

Thanks to my involvement in many extracurricular activities throughout my time in college, like working in the admissions office and serving in student government, I held a front-row seat to the behind-the-scenes efforts undertaken by university administrators and faculty on a daily basis. In this book, you'll read the stories most college administrators, faculty members, and professors hope you never hear about—because if more students shared their everyday college stories like mine, it very well might completely crumble the foundation of institutional power of America's colleges and universities. It's time for America to hear the truth—the good, the bad, and the ugly—if we are to make a vital change for Gen Z and those attending college after us who want to become our next generation of leaders.

My experience is the tip of the iceberg. In fact, millions of Americans like me endure the dystopian reality of a college campus every day, especially conservative students who are willing to risk it all by publicly sharing their conservative identities. They challenge other students and even faculty members to embrace the intellectual freedom that allows us to have a peaceful exchange of ideas. We are quite literally fighting an intellectual war for the future of our nation and world.

In this war, our college campuses are the front line. If the leaders of our generation (and truthfully, all Americans of all ages) are not willing to stand up and push back against the leftist chokehold on America's universities, no one will, and this apathy will yield consequences far graver than losing our college campuses. We'll lose the freedom we were born into as Americans. Our country is truly the last stand on earth for Western civilization, individual liberty, and freedom from an overly oppressive government. If we fail to recognize the exceptionality of the American experiment and carry freedom into the next generation, we are boarding a one-way train toward full-blown socialism (which, by the way, is taught as an optimal reality on many campuses and is favored over capitalism by many young Americans, according to CNBC[3]).

My hope is that this book will make you smile (and perhaps even laugh) at the absurdity of today's American college experience. But more so, I hope these words reveal that America's young adults, Gen Z, are in desperate need of a single thing—*truth*. There has perhaps never been a time in global history where young people must filter the difference between fact and fiction so frequently and in such a complex way. For college students, it's not just in the media—it's on our final exams, overheard among friends, and uttered from our professors. If our nation is to succeed throughout the next generation, America's colleges and universities are in desperate need of a reality check.

---

3   Kathleen Elkins, "Most young Americans prefer socialism to capitalism, new report finds," *CNBC*, last modified August 7, 2018, https://www.cnbc.com/2018/08/14/fewer-than-half-of-young-americans-are-positive-about-capitalism.html.

CHAPTER ONE

. . . .

INDOCTRINATION 101

*"My generation did this to you! I am devastated about the future of our world! If you're an immigrant, you will be deported! Students of color are in grave danger! Trump is **literally Hitler**!"*

—CSU SPANISH PROFESSOR, NOVEMBER 2016

On November 9, 2016, I heard those words in my classroom, and my jaw hit the floor. It was the day after the 2016 presidential election, one of the most polarizing nights in our nation's history. I had just sat down for my first class. What I had assumed would be any other day soon turned out to be a turning point in my college experience. I was about to experience the first of many instances when my professors would use their platform and status to openly and shamelessly indoctrinate students.

My Spanish language professor slumped into our Spanish Medical Terminology course ten minutes late. She was sobbing uncontrollably and dressed head-to-toe in black, complete with a lace veil artfully draped over her face. (Sorry—I shouldn't have assumed her gender. More on that later.) Her attire symbolized a funeral to grieve the "death of our nation," as she would put it moments later. She promptly announced—in English, I might add—we wouldn't be completing any Spanish coursework. Instead, we'd use the remaining forty minutes to discuss the election in a "safe space." She then quickly apologized for the results of the vote. "I know it's none of your faults. *My* generation did this to you, and I have no idea how we will ever repay you," she said.

I nearly burst into laughter. *Everyone must think this is crazy,* I thought.

But after I looked around the room, I realized every other student was somberly nodding in almost robotic fashion. They were eager to say or do anything to impress the person who controlled their grade. *Really*?!

For the remainder of class, students shared anecdotes about how they "feared for their lives" as undocumented students; how they were "terrified" to leave their dorm rooms because of "racist Republicans" patrolling campus; or how they needed psychological counseling to deal with the emotional trauma of Donald Trump's election. (So much for my feeling of elation that we elected a truly conservative president.)

Maybe my Spanish class is being dramatic, I thought. Surely, this was an isolated incident. Unfortunately, this class proved to set the tone for the day.

I soon discovered this would not be just a comical story from a single class I'd call home to tell my parents about—this would encompass every class of my day. Two more of my professors showed up in their funeral garb. (Had they made calls to one another the night before to coordinate their dress code?) Plus, every professor canceled their class material to discuss the traumatic aftermath of the election. They blamed their own generation. They shared how they all "knew" that none of their students or peer professors voted for Donald Trump. Rather, some ambiguous group of middle America, white racists from "their generation" was responsible for his election. (I guess everyone forgot that Fort Collins, Colorado is about as middle America as a college town can get.)

By the end of the day, I was shocked. Not only was I angry that I had actually paid for "class" that day, but I also realized how truly isolated I felt as a conservative college student. In every classroom, I could barely hold back my laughter for the insanity of the words uttered by my professors. As their heads exploded with rage, they literally compared the newly elected president to Adolph Hitler, offered students indefinite extensions on assignments and exams, and angrily screamed about the dangerous evils that conservatives pose to my generation.

I could barely hold back my laughter while listening to my professors, but simultaneously, I was heartbroken. Almost every student in each class was either in tears themselves or enthusiastically hanging on to every biased word that came out of these professors' mouths. My fellow students, not to mention the outraged professors, would have been shocked to discover a nineteen-year-old, female, conservative student sitting in their midst, quite elated by the outcome of the election. I had not yet found my political courage; I was still reserved about my conservative beliefs. So, in each class, I sat quietly and looked down at my textbooks to hide my amusement (and shock) until the day was finished.

I knew students in other fields—particularly in the political sciences or ethnic studies—experienced political bias in their classrooms. But I was studying Spanish Language and Biomedical Sciences. In a Spanish language or chemistry class, it should be difficult for a professor to insert political biases into the material, given how these courses are graded by multiple-choice exams or vocabulary quizzes. After all, how political can you get when analyzing the human renal system or conjugating Spanish verbs?

Prior to President Trump's election, I hadn't personally witnessed professors using their platform to indoctrinate students in my classes. However, the day after the 2016 presidential election, it occurred to me that not one of my professors had shared my political and personal values. That's when I realized my instructors *had* been indoctrinating students all along, even in nuanced ways that were not immediately or obviously visible from the student's perspective. From that day forward, I observed that nearly every one of my college courses were wrought with my professors' personal political biases—even in the hard sciences, where you'd think the materials were based on science and taught from an unbiased perspective. In my human gross anatomy course, for example, my male professor explained during the course of evolution when humans evolved from apes that humans had simply and spontaneously *developed* a frontal lobe of their brain "just because." He followed this with a snide statement of, "Unless you believe in creation instead of evolution," the male professor added with a wink. The three hundred students present that day snickered while apparently hanging on his every word, eager to impress the person controlling their grade. Regardless of one's personal religious beliefs, or even the option that creation and evolution worked together throughout human history, only one viewpoint was presented as "fact."

Similarly, my physiology professor painstakingly spent weeks explaining how a human infant is beautifully developed from fertilization through birth, sharing intricate details about their unique DNA, heartbeat, and survival in their mother's womb. Yet, this same professor finished the unit by explaining how abortion is *not* killing a human—a statement that students accepted as fact, as, again, their grades hung in the balance. Later, I was faced with a multiple-choice final exam question in my eukaryotic cellular biology course, which looked something like the following.

Select the true statement:

a. All life evolved from a single prokaryotic cell billions of years ago.
b. God created the universe.
c. Eukaryotic and prokaryotic cells are the same.
d. None of the above.

(The correct answer was a.)

Still, perhaps the most blatant expression of political bias came on the first day of my senior year during my Population Health and Disease Prevention course. Within the first twenty minutes of class, my professor (whom I'll call Dr. Teague) said this, verbatim:

"Trump is a dipshit and the worst president we've ever had when it comes to public health. If you're really into economics and you're a rich person, he's a great president, but when it comes to public health, he's the worst. Obama was better, not perfect, but better. I guess that's the difference between Democrats and Republicans—Democrats care about everyone, and Republicans only care about some people."

Yikes. Truly, a student's political affiliation should have nothing to do with their competence to improve public health policy—which was, of course, the supposed objective of the course. My professor, on the other hand, seemed to believe our course was directly centered around one's political party of choice and that conservative students like myself did not belong in the business of "helping people," particularly when it came to public health. I swallowed very hard.

Later, I took a quiz in the same course that asked me to identify "three pros to Obamacare" and "three disadvantages of the current US healthcare system." We were not asked to identify any cons of Obamacare nor possible advantages to our nation's advanced healthcare system. Acceptable answers to the first question included: "insurance for everyone" and "more money in the healthcare system thanks to taxes." My answer, "countering the costs of insurance companies," was marked incorrect. Similarly, I received no points on the latter question with my answer "lack of healthcare price transparency," despite my significant experience researching public health for educational and professional experiences, while a correct answer included "doctors want you sick" (apparently so they can enjoy a steady stream of business). Before the quiz, students were never provided with lecture notes or study guides. When I pressed Dr. Teague about why we faced these subjective questions on the quiz, he shared that in his eyes, my answers weren't the most important answers despite their possibility of being factually correct. I received a 65 percent—a D—for the quiz, which accounted for a significant portion of my grade. Yikes again!

But Dr. Teague wasn't done. During one of the final classes of the semester, he walked toward my seat and quietly said, "We are beginning class today by discussing immigration."

I looked at him, thinking, *Okay,* ***why*** *am I your private audience?*

"I expect some comments out of you," he continued. "Don't disappoint me."

From my point of view, I had been singled out as the sole conservative student willing to present opposing views. I quickly prepared. I began furiously writing down facts about illegal immigration to counter the leftist narrative my professor was sure to propagate in the coming minutes. I included sources, data, and general arguments for strengthening legal immigration versus opening our borders. I was ready to fight for conservative principles, even in the presence of my peers.

Dr. Teague began the conversation by showing a PowerPoint slide. It was empty, except for the following:

"The country is full. We don't want you here. Please stay away."
—President Trump

Dr. Teague went on to explain how this statement was recently uttered by President Trump at the southern border. Skeptical of the validity of this statement (as for all I know, my professor could have made it up), I eagerly awaited his next move.

He asked, "Should we close our borders? Literally, at some point, we will be full—are we there now? What do you think about this [statement]? First, the students who are for this, please speak up. You're not *wrong;* you just have a different opinion than most other people in this class. Does anybody want to support this?"

Taking in the condescending tone of his question, I was sure students would be too afraid to speak up. Surprisingly, several students did, only to be met with direct opposition from Dr. Teague.

One student stated, "I go both ways with it because I have a family member who was killed by an illegal immigrant, so [this issue] gets kind of personal with me."

Our professor immediately responded, "First of all, I'm sorry. But the first point is, you had a friend or a family member who was killed by an illegal immigrant. Uh, I, uh, again, I'm sorry, but I'm not sure that's an argument against illegal immigrants. That's an argument against *bad people*, and this one just *happened* to be an illegal immigrant."

My professor combatted his student's firsthand experience of the negative consequences of illegal immigration by discrediting his argument altogether. Now, I was even more eager to join the conversation. I raised my hand and asked about the source of the President Trump quote.

"That's a great question," my professor responded. "He was

standing at the border and there were, there was a lot of context, and he actually made this statement, basically paraphrased about four times—you know, he likes to repeat himself for emphasis, um, but he, the statement was that he wanted to completely close the border. Somebody asked him the question about, 'Do you mean to immigrants or do you mean to traffic in general?' And he made...this was his response to that question."

Clearly, my professor was uninterested in providing any evidence whatsoever that the statement had actually been uttered, as he failed to provide a source or any news article linked to the three sentences he had boldly displayed on the board.

I was interested in the facts. I pointed out how misleading it is to paraphrase three short sentences and deliver them as if they were a direct quote. (By that point, I wasn't shy about my beliefs. I had seen President Trump speak on a number of occasions, had interned in the Trump White House, and had frequently heard President Trump and his administration advocate for legal immigration.) In fact, under the leadership of President Donald Trump prior to the COVID-19 pandemic, our nation had more vacant jobs than people who could fill them. So, we need legal immigration to be economically successful.

Eager to "not let my professor down," I continued sharing the truth of our southern border by informing my professor and classmates about the health risks of illegal immigration across the southern border, namely drug trafficking, human trafficking, and sexual assault, all affecting the lives of immigrants and citizens alike. After all, this class was titled "Population Health and Disease Prevention," so I figured while we were talking about illegal immigration, we may as well consider it within the context of population health. I gave a number of facts and statistics: 70 percent of women and children crossing the southern border were sexually and/or physically assaulted as of January 2019.[4] Also, in fiscal year 2017, Immigration and Customs Enforcement seized over 2,300 pounds of fentanyl at the southern border—enough to kill every individual in the United States.[5]

Of course, my professor was quick to discredit anything and everything offered by a conservative voice in his classroom.

"Kay. Two reactions to that," my professor sharply remarked. "Many actually, and I'm sure other people do too. We're *not talking* about drug trafficking. Certainly, it's a related problem, but, and if we keep mixing drug trafficking in with sex trafficking, then yes, it becomes a much, much bigger conversation. This statement and the conversation we're having so far is about immigration *only*. Certainly, Americans bring in drugs, too, so closing the border wouldn't mean no one could come in or go out. The other thing I'll tell you is you didn't like the source of this quote because I didn't give you a source. Um, other people, myself included, would be equally skeptical with, you said 2,300 and 70 percent coming straight from the White House itself. Whoever did this [statement] is probably full of shit, so is the White House sometimes. So, all sources of our information should be checked."

4   "The Crisis at the Southern Border Is Too Urgent to Ignore," *The White House*, last modified January 10, 2019, https://www.whitehouse.gov/briefings-statements/crisis-southern-border-urgent-ignore/.

5   Ibid.

The truth behind these conversations always comes out eventually. In this case, the broad topic of illegal immigration was perfectly pertinent to the topic of "population health." That is, until the statistics failed to fit the narrative propagated by my professor, who quickly discredited the relationship of drug trafficking, sex trafficking, and immigration, since he moved on from the subject as soon as (*Gasp!*) a student shared legitimate reasons against illegal immigration from a health perspective.

The day after our lively exchange, Dr. Teague stated—in front of the class—"Isabel, are you going to go off again, or can I leave the door open?" before laughing and adding, "I'm just teasing."

I'm sure he *was* just teasing, and I had grown a thick skin during my four years at CSU. Still, for students who had yet to establish firm conservative beliefs or who hadn't found their voice, my professor's behavior likely scared them out of vocalizing their conservative opinions.

Make no mistake, political, religious, and personal values invariably found their way into even my hard sciences courses, which are supposedly preparing students for medical or veterinary school. In complete disregard of what any of their students may believe, professors will espouse their personal (invariably leftist) positions. You don't need to take a political or gender studies class to confront this reality. It's quickly becoming commonplace in every class on every campus in America.

CHAPTER TWO

· · · · · · · · · · · · · · · · · ·

IT'S NOT JUST ME

"God, the Easter Bunny, and Santa Claus are all in the same category. Don't try to prove me wrong—this is how my course will run."

—CSU Philosophy Professor

As I navigated professor bias in my classes and on assignments, I couldn't believe I was the *only* student feeling isolated and silenced on campus. As I looked further into the leftist indoctrination of the college classroom, I discovered that the other 33,000 students at CSU were experiencing comparable (or even worse) situations in their classrooms a few buildings away. I was often informed by my friends in the political science department that students were (and still are) taught in their political science courses that capitalism is a failed system designed to keep minorities in poverty, and socialism is the greatest governmental and economic structure ever invented. It's even taught that conservatism is a façade for the racial supremacy of rich white men. Meanwhile, *The Communist Manifesto* remains required reading for many courses in the political science department. In fact, you'd be hard-pressed to find even one professor who's willing to declare that capitalism has lifted more individuals out of poverty than any other system on earth.[6]

If a student ever dares to confront the leftist agenda during class time, their professors target them by giving them a failing grade on an assignment or humiliating them in front of their peers in the classroom. For the record, this targeting does *not* only happen to conservative students.

One of my left-leaning friends at CSU, whom I'll call Maria, even experienced ideology-based discrimination in her Queer Expressions course (yes, that's the class title!).

When asked about whether traditionally all-female colleges and universities should accept transgender females (that is, a male transitioning to become a female), she replied that while other educational institutions absolutely should do so, traditionally, female universities hail as a beacon for feminist causes and strong female students to become leaders. She shared that her experience as a feminist woman had much to do with the fact that she was a biological woman—she possessed the capability of creating life and sharing that particular gift with the world—while transgender women have a different biological experience. Upon hearing this answer, her classmates and professor rebuked her words. They called her "insensitive" and "hateful" for being so oppressive and opined that her thoughts didn't actually matter on the subject because she was white and not a woman of color—never mind the fact she is a disabled lesbian woman. I suppose you need a minimum number of

---

6   Robert P. Murphy, "Extreme Poverty Rates Plummet Under Capitalism," *Foundation for Economic Equality,* last modified May 30, 2018, https://fee.org/articles/extreme-poverty-rates-plummet-under-capitalism/.

supposed "oppressed" identities for your opinion to actually matter in the gender studies department?

Perhaps the greatest level of prejudice propagated by CSU faculty is that of religious, or more correctly, *anti*-religious, bias. During her second year at CSU, my friend, Angelica (not her real name) enrolled in an Introduction to Philosophy course to fulfill a degree requirement. She faced a real-life experience running deeply parallel to the fictional Christian movie, *God's Not Dead*. During the first day of the semester, the professor matter-of-factly stated, "God, the Easter Bunny, and Santa Claus are all in the same category. Don't try to prove me wrong—this is how my course will run."

Later in the semester, while discussing belief in a higher power, the professor instructed his students to write a paper using social consciousness and logical evidence to prove God is not real. This paper accounted for one-third of their grade. Students were not offered an opportunity to write a paper proving the opposite; they were forced to state God is not real.

Angelica, a devout Christian whose family emigrated from the Middle East to freely practice Christianity, was infuriated. She confronted her professor during office hours and asked to write a paper on why she firmly believed God was real.

The professor's response?

He was initially amazed that she had the audacity to believe in God at all. Secondly, he was shocked by her proposal. He explained that if she wrote from her perspective, she would be ignoring the assignment's instruction to use evidence because, as he noted, there is no evidence supporting God's existence. Consequently, he informed her that she would fail the assignment and the entire course.

After many lengthy and intense arguments with the professor, including the threat of a lawsuit, he eventually permitted her to write the paper from her perspective—provided that she wrote her paper three times longer than everyone else's. Likely, there were other Christian students in the course who lacked Angelica's courage and felt forced to write the original paper out of fear of failing. To this day, that breaks my heart.

These are a few of the stories from my campus that will never make the news. They may lead you to believe that CSU is nothing but a hotbed for leftist causes propagated by agenda-driven professors and administration. To some degree, that is true. Yet, it's not unique to Fort Collins, Colorado. The *Econ Journal Watch* performed a study in 2016 of more than 7,000 acting university professors in various fields throughout the country; the ratio of liberal to conservative professors was nearly twelve to one.[7] Remember, we aren't simply discussing support staff, such as administrators, janitors, or cooks. We're talking about the individuals who teach thousands of college students on campuses across America. Often, these professors teach in fields completely unrelated to politics, yet their nearly uniform political bias almost always finds a way into their classrooms. Instead of

---

7   Mitchell Langbert, Anthony J. Quain, and Daniel B. Klein, "Faculty Voter Registration in Economics, History, Journalism, Law, and Psychology," *Character Issues* 13, no. 3 (September 2016): 422–451, https://econjwatch.org/articles/faculty-voter-registration-in-economics-history-journalism-communications-law-and-psychology.

preparing our nation's young adults for success in the real world, colleges are charging thousands of dollars to students (and their parents) to hear their chemistry or journalism professor's opinion on immigration, abortion, or an upcoming election.

I'm not the only one to point out the one-sided political influence found on college campuses. Even professors feel this tension.

Dr. Samuel Abrams, a professor of political science at Sarah Lawrence College, understands firsthand the extreme ratio of liberal to conservative professors on campuses, as Dr. Abrams is a conservative-leaning political science professor. Seeing a lack of data on other college faculty, he felt compelled to study what percentage of college administrators and staff members, *other* than professors, identified as liberal or left-leaning. In 2018, Abrams surveyed over 900 "student-facing" administrators, whose work focuses on the student experience on campus. The survey revealed that only 6 percent of administrators identified as conservative to even the slightest degree, while 71 percent self-identified as liberal or very liberal. This 2018 study was truly the first of its kind in examining the extreme leftist bias among university faculty and details the important reality of the skew of progressively-minded faculty and staff at our nation's universities.

* * *

If a conservative-leaning student enrolls at a university, they are quickly "outed" as such, as college professors often insert a socially divisive educational curriculum that directly exposes a student's conservative identity. Professors often host classroom activities supposedly intended to promote "diversity" and discuss the all-important topic of "social justice." In reality, these activities serve as mechanisms to point out differences among students—not so that we may overcome these differences, but so that some students will be directly targeted because of them. I experienced this in my Psychology 100 course when I went on a "privilege walk," which is an increasingly common activity in classes, extracurriculars, and jobs on college campuses. In our lecture hall designed for a few hundred students, the professor instructed the students to line up at the back of the room. She informed us of the rules of the exercise: she would read off a litany of statements about identity. Then, each student would take a respective number of steps forward or backward if that statement applied to them. The wall was the starting point, where we were all considered equal, and no student had an unfair advantage.

Our young, female, white professor began reading statements about identity and instructed us to move either forward or backward, respectively. Some of her instructions included, "If you have blonde hair, take two steps forward. If you are graduating with debt, take ten steps backward. If you are studying to be a doctor or a lawyer, take three steps forward. If you are of a minority race, take twelve steps backward. If you showered before coming to class this morning, take one step forward."

Here's one of my personal favorites, "If you voted for and support President Donald Trump, take six steps forward."

The instructor explained that the further forward a student

traveled during her instructions, the more societal "privilege" the student has, giving them a predisposed advantage toward success. As each moved up or down the spectrum, my fellow students looked around the room, some with shame, others with pride, but all very confused with the exercise. Most students actively participated, and some were even brave enough to reveal intimate details about themselves. (I will never forget the look of disgust from my professor as I proudly stepped forward to reveal that I had voted for and supported President Trump. You could hear a pin drop in the lecture hall.)

At the conclusion of the exercise, only a handful of students remained at the back of the classroom—most of us were randomly scattered throughout the room to represent our various levels of "privilege." (Never mind that everyone present was a college student with the same opportunity to work hard toward success.) Our professor ended by stating, "This is how unfair America is."

This activity was not designed to teach students about psychology, how our minds work, or how to promote a psychologically healthy lifestyle. Rather, it was a vehicle for which our outwardly leftist professor could pit students against one another to further her own political agenda. (As a side note, I always scratch my head over activities like this. If it *really* provided so many advantages to be blonde and an outspoken supporter of President Trump, why wouldn't everyone *want* to dye their hair and support him?)

Activities like the privilege walk occur every day on college campuses. As a result, students are pitted against one another. Those with "oppressive identities," like white skin, economic security, and a conservative voting record, must out themselves in front of their peers to remind everyone that some have inherent advantages over others, regardless of how hard an individual is willing to work. If this sounds ridiculous to you—good. These curriculum modules are past the point of insanity and do nothing to further a student's education.

What does this mean for students? If they uphold their own personal integrity and hold true to their own belief systems—political, religious, or otherwise—they are subject to academic punishment. This disproportionately affects conservative students. And it's not about one grade; it's about their entire GPA. If a professor fails a student because of their beliefs (as Angelica's professor threatened to do), that would fundamentally alter the student's GPA. While in school, your GPA affects nearly every aspect of your life, from scholarship funding and graduate school admission to leadership positions on campus (like student body president). If we are truly passionate about providing the strongest possible education to all hard-working students regardless of their personal or political backgrounds, something *must* change.

Dennis Prager, a popular conservative writer, radio show host, young adult mentor, and Co-Founder and President of PragerU (an organization that introduces Americans to conservative ideas through video content), addresses this issue head-on. He says students should never compromise their personal values for a better grade. His understanding of the current climate of today's college classroom is profound when it comes to the dedication of America's leftist college professors who indoctrinate students to believe in the leftist agenda. While speaking at a political function in 2019, Dennis said, "If your child did not come home from college stupid, it was either luck or [because] they were drunk for four years. I see a silver lining with drunk college students, because at least [then] they weren't indoctrinated!" In response, the crowd laughed, but for Dennis and millions of contemporary college students, this is no laughing matter. Dennis went on to proclaim, "Today, sending your child to college is playing Russian roulette with their values."

This quote struck a chord with me because it is saturated with truth. Far too often, the indoctrination that seeps into our college classrooms affects students on a much deeper level than through their GPA—although that in and of itself is vitally important for laying the foundation of one's future. Often, if a conservative student questions or challenges the leftist agenda put forth by their professor, they will not only receive a poor grade, but they will also be socially humiliated and outed by their peers as an "evil" conservative for doing so.

Professors are exceptionally successful at creating an army of students who will fight for leftist causes if only to receive praise or admiration in the eyes of the authority figures on campus. Risking your social reputation in the name of your values for a college course is an incredibly dangerous thing to do. However, it's of more dire concern when students are often silenced into submission out of fear before they even get a chance to stand up for their values. Most conservative students refuse to speak up because they don't want to risk their academic careers and social lives.

Due to the overwhelming leftist skew at colleges, professors assume that even if a conservative student is in their classroom, they will be silent about their beliefs and will never challenge the authority of the professor simply out of fear. In most cases, the assumption is true—rarely will students knowingly opt for a bad grade or social humiliation for standing up to a professor. As a result, professors freely proclaim and execute their leftist agenda without fear of retaliation—and the cycle continues.

Universities and the media won't expose any of this. However, at this very moment, biased, leftist professors are directly targeting conservative students in their classrooms. These professors are determined to silence and intimidate conservatives from ever speaking out.

You'd think that it couldn't get much worse than that, but you haven't seen anything yet.

CHAPTER THREE

· · · · · · · · · · · · · · · · · · · ·

SOCIALISM SUCKS

"Why does the United States hate equality? Why can't we implement socialism to make sure all people are truly equal?"
—CSU STUDENTS STUDYING ABROAD IN CUBA, SPRING 2016

I will never forget what it felt like to touch socialism, to see it up close, to witness crumbling buildings and rotting food sold to people living in abject poverty. To be interrogated by government officials at the airport and ignored by our government tour guide. I will never forget my visit to Cuba.

Prior to the 2016 election-induced funeral in my classes, I had only experienced one blatant example of indoctrination taking place at CSU. As a freshman Spanish student, I took advantage of the many study abroad programs offered during spring break—I had the unique privilege of traveling to Cuba in March of 2016 prior to the allowance of commercial travel to the island. Interestingly, the day our student group returned to the United States was the day President Barack Obama arrived in Havana for his historic visit, which led to an unprecedented scale back of restrictions against the communist regime.

My 2016 visit to Cuba offered a unique opportunity for any American, but particularly for a college student living on a campus hailing socialism as the ideal system of government, to experience what Cuba was truly like on the ground. Prior to arriving, I had conducted several internet searches about where I would be traveling. The media and the establishment Left told me I would arrive in a tropical paradise with stunning old cars, pristine beaches, and sprawling resorts. But I understood that I would be traveling to a socialist nation. I logically knew that Cuba was home to intense poverty, and from the comfort of the United States, though, I couldn't wrap my head around what I would experience. Until the plane touched down in Havana, there was no way I could have fully understood the reality of socialism.

Over the span of ten days, our group traveled throughout the capital city of Havana and a remote region known as Pinar del Rio, and we experienced the elusive Cuban culture for ourselves. Importantly, the trip was led by two CSU professors from the ethnic studies department, and students were given class credit if they wrote a paper about the trip after we returned to campus. Knowing the rumors and jokes of extreme leftist bias in ethnic studies departments across the nation, I knew the experience was likely to lean significantly to the left side of the aisle. What I was unprepared for, however, was the exorbitant number of blatant lies told to students on the trip by Cuban tour guides *and* our professors. Many of my peers blindly accepted these lies as truth, regardless of what they witnessed in Cuba. As the youngest participant on a college trip with mostly juniors and seniors, I knew this wasn't merely immaturity from naïve teenagers. Years of calculated indoctrination created their biased view.

Before our departure to Havana, we engaged in group meetings intended to prepare us for the extreme culture shock we were about to experience. Our professors explained the only way an American university group could travel inside Cuba was to obtain a special educational visa and be assigned a government-employed tour guide and chauffeur. We would most likely be unable to travel anywhere without our tour guide, and most of our trips each day would consist of visiting government-owned and operated facilities. Our teacher also prepped us for extensive questioning by border patrol agents at the airport. We were informed that government officials would keep a close eye on our American university group since it appeared only three American groups were allowed in the nation at the same time.

Truthfully, engaging in these predeparture briefings barely prepared me for what I was about to experience.

The moment our plane touched down in Havana, it became clear that our group of American students would fail to stay under the radar during our Cuban immersion—government officials instantly and intensively questioned us at the airport regarding the purpose of our visit as our passports were stamped at customs. I quickly aroused the suspicion of immigration officers when I greeted them in Spanish. I received excessive questioning and interrogation. Why could I speak Spanish? Did I know anyone in the country? Would I be visiting anyone specific? Did I bring a camera or audiovisual equipment into the country? Even my small hand-held GoPro camera became questionable. Suddenly, I understood—compared to the United States, this was an opposite universe.

As our bus pulled away from the airport, I had the sense that I had stepped back in time, and not necessarily in the glamorous, nostalgic way. I instantly observed the lack of private industry. There didn't appear to be any companies advertising their products on buildings or signs. Old cars and crumbling infrastructure met me at every turn as we drove past dozens of state-sponsored billboards sporting socialist propaganda, such as *La Revolución Seguira Adelante* (loose translation: "The revolution still continues," referring to an ongoing push for socialism in Cuba). Stray dogs and skinny children were scattered alongside the main road, many playing soccer and waving to our bus.

Our government-issued tour guide spoke over the loudspeaker touting seemingly impressive statistics about the infrastructure and history of Havana (in the 1950s, revolutionaries sought to overthrow President Batista to implement a new structure of government along Marxist lines—and the Communist Party rose to power). With a smile on her face, our tour guide explained the importance of this revolution. She paused to underline the equality of all Cuban citizens under the resulting communist government. Apparently, this equality ensured that all Cubans have equal access to education and healthcare, the government's two most important services. In fact, our guide informed the group that the government was then spending nearly all its budget on those two industries. This had, in her words, led to impressive educational growth in the nation and had eliminated the problem of only the wealthy being able to access quality healthcare. Moreover, every Cuban had a place to call home through the government's universal housing initiative. The government had established the principle of income equity for all Cubans following the revolution—a doctor, a lawyer, and a restaurant dishwasher all had virtually the same income.

I made a mental note to later ask everyday Cubans about these talking points.

Our bus pulled into the parking lot of La Plaza de la Revolución, or Revolution Square, an eleven-acre piece of land consisting of bland, gray buildings. As we climbed off the bus, our guide informed us that Revolution Square was home to a handful of the most important government buildings in the nation, and the Castro brothers owned several houses there. Towering over the square along the façade of one of the buildings was a massive metal art piece depicting Cuban Revolution leader and socialism icon Che Guevara. As my classmates marveled at the mural, I heard the hushed excitement from one of them, who was sporting a Che Guevara T-shirt. Some were ecstatic to see such a large tribute to a man who, in their eyes and the eyes of the Cuban government, was nothing less than a hero.

I felt my stomach turn.

I had conducted research of my own on Guevara prior to our arrival in the nation and knew that he was no hero for the poor and marginalized—he was nothing short of a murderous villain. What my classmates had seemingly failed to learn during their three or four years at CSU was the inconvenient history of this troubled individual, one that didn't fit the narrative their professors or peers wanted them to believe. I could spend pages discussing the truth behind Che Guevara. Instead, I'll let Guevara's oft-repeated quotes speak for him:

"A revolutionary must become a cold killing machine moti-vated by pure hate."

He was well-known for executing his political or ideological opponents, opposed a free press, and even forced homosex-ual individuals into forced labor camps.[8] This was my peers' *hero*—the man they touted as an advocate for "true" equality. Give me a break.

As our first day in Havana continued, we drove through countless neighborhoods filled with high-rise buildings. They looked like something out of a war zone. Windows and doors were missing from apartments; floors and walls were crumbling to dust. Our guide quietly mentioned to one of my professors that, on average, three buildings in Havana fall down because of infrastructure failure...*per day*. This wasn't the picturesque wonderland I had searched on the internet. This was a decaying wasteland. I supposed infra-structure failure was one of many consequences of having no national private wealth to maintain these buildings. When the government spent nearly 100 percent of its budget on education and healthcare, there would not be much left over for everyday structural maintenance.

I raised my hand and asked our guide how many people lived in one apartment at a time, given she had mentioned univer-sal housing in Cuba. Amazingly, I never got an answer. She simply turned away as if she hadn't heard my question and proceeded to share more (likely prescribed) talking points. I later discovered that an entire extended family—a dozen people or more—often live in a single, crumbling, miniscule

---

8   Maxim Lott, "5 Inconvenient Truths about Che Guevara," last modified February 18, 2019, https://www.foxnews.com/politics/5-inconvenient-truths-about-che-guevara.

apartment that we would consider structurally uninhabitable in America. So much for universal housing.

For lunch and dinner on that first day, our guide escorted us to fancy restaurants known as *paladares,* the small contingent of restaurants that are not owned or operated by the Cuban government. These businesses began in 1993 after the government legalized a very small number of private business operations in the hospitality industry. They served only a handful of people and functioned inside the business owner's home.[9] Later, when I ate at a number of other *paladares*, it became clear the Cuban government didn't want American students eating in publicly operated restaurants with meal rations and limited ingredients.

While eating a delicious dinner at *La Paladar de San Cristobal*—one of the most famous restaurants in Cuba—I noticed photos on the walls of celebrities and public figures from around the world documenting their visits. The owner was particularly proud of a photo of Beyoncé taken when she visited the restaurant. Hearing his stories, I began to understand why my perception of Cuba—before the trip—was so different. American celebrities and global public figures didn't experience the real Cuba, just as I likely wouldn't during our visit. Like me, they were served the finest foods in the nation, stayed in safe and clean hotels, and largely avoided the inconvenience of extreme poverty caused by complete government control. Alongside my classmates, they wore blindfolds to the realities of socialism.

---

9   Patty Diez, "Inside 'Paladares,' a Revealing Look at Cuba's Underground
    Restaurant Culture," *Eater*, last modified November 28, 2017, https://www.eater.
    com/2017/11/28/16552884/paladares-cuban-cookbook-plantain-chips-recipe.

I began my second day in Cuba by wandering off the beaten path to attend Catholic Mass with two of our chaperones. I was the only college student who wanted to attend (big surprise there). Growing up Catholic, I had made it a point to (at least try to) attend Mass in every foreign country I visited. I loved hearing the same readings all around the world and reciting the same prayers in different languages. It gave me a feeling of connection to thousands of people halfway around the world. Truthfully, given the few stories I'd heard on the news regarding the government's intolerance of the Christian faith, I was surprised to find an operational parish in Cuba, but I did, nonetheless.

Less than a dozen people from around town attended Mass, and as the blonde-haired, blue-eyed American, I stuck out like a sore thumb. Following the service, I was approached by a handful of older women who asked where I was from and why I was visiting Cuba. When I answered with the word "America," they got stars in their eyes. They simply couldn't believe that I was from the United States or that I had gone out of my way to experience the real Cuba, the one the government didn't want me to see, by sitting with them in church. This was the first prolonged interaction I had with native Cubans, and it would not be the last.

Like most buildings I had seen in Havana, the church was crumbling. Large chunks of the exterior façade appeared to be missing, and the building blended in with its surroundings as a bland shade of gray. Inside, a beautiful hand-painted mural of Christ surrounded by angels and saints lined the ceiling, and carefully-placed stained glass windows adorned a wall. In contrast to this serenity, revolution-era bullet holes and cracks in the walls punctured the scene. The stark contrast between the expected physical beauty of a church and the harsh visualizations of socialism continue to haunt my memory.

As I joined my classmates for the remainder of the day, I felt truly sorry they had missed the opportunity to get a glimpse of the real Cuba. I asked questions that our tour guide would have simply ignored and got real answers from kind and warm people. I had witnessed the awe the Cuban people have for the freedom promised to Americans as our birthright. I silently made a deal with myself to quietly break the rules a few more times during my trip and see more of the real Cuba. I was determined to experience the reality of this complex nation.

Our second day in Cuba was, as expected, scripted to perfection. We wandered the streets of *La Habana Vieja* (Old Havana), which was once home to the historic district of the city but had evolved into the tourist center. Hundreds of foreign tourists, but very few Americans, dotted the streets and dashed in and out of restaurants and shops. Unlike where I had attended Mass, the buildings in Old Havana were painted to perfection in bright, fun colors. No bullet holes, no exterior façades. Street performers—employed by the Cuban government, my guide informed me—wore stilts and elaborate costumes as they danced to Latin music. Birds chirped, children ate ice cream, and everyone snapped photos. *This* was the Cuba I had seen on the internet.

Toward the end of our stop in Old Havana, I noticed a large crew of workers power washing the colorful buildings and, oddly, painting the sidewalks. For a country experiencing such extreme infrastructure failure, this seemed strange, so I asked our guide about it. She responded that the President of the United States—Barack Obama—was planning to visit Cuba at the end of the week for his historic summit. The government, she said, was knee-deep in preparations for his arrival. For the most part, Old Havana was the only small area of the country the president would visit. At this, I chuckled. *Of course* the government would go to extreme lengths to ensure their crumbling socialist nation looked pristine. After all, a sitting US president had not traveled to Cuba since President Calvin Coolidge in 1928! I wondered what lengths the regime would go to hide the horrors of socialism from the world and prayed President Obama would not be so naïve to think the real Cuba mirrored dressed-up Old Havana.

Our afternoon continued with a guided tour at the Museum of the Revolution, which quickly became one of the most impactful experiences I had during my time in Cuba. Housed in the pre-revolution presidential palace, the museum offers a slanted history of the victory won by Che Guevara and the Castro brothers. It perfectly illustrates the government's attitude toward America. Of course, I assumed the government museum would have an obvious agenda, but I was unprepared for what I experienced.

Alongside heroic tributes to Che Guevara, Raul Castro, and Fidel Castro, the museum houses a substantial collection of anti-American propaganda. Exhibits condemn the United States for issuing an embargo against Cuba. Another installation identifies specific US presidents who had treated the nation harshly in the past; grotesque cartoons compare them to corrupt public figures throughout history. President Ronald Reagan is depicted as an ugly cowboy alongside a placard that reads, "Thanks you cretin for helped [sic] us to STRENGTHEN THE REVOLUTION." President George H.W. Bush, depicted as an angry Roman gladiator, stands next to a placard which reads, "Thanks you cretin for helped [sic] us to CONSOLIDATE THE REVOLUTION." Finally, President George W. Bush, depicted wearing a Nazi helmet and holding a book about Cuban freedom upside down, stands beside a placard which reads, "Thanks you cretin for helped [sic] us TO MAKE SOCIALISM IRREVOCABLE."

Most of my classmates snickered at these drawings. They especially got a kick out of President George W. Bush's Nazi garb, and some praised the implementation of socialism despite the United States' attempts to prevent it. Again, I felt my stomach turning.

Our tour through the museum eventually led us outside, where a massive armory featuring weapons from the revolution and even missiles from the Cuban Missile Crisis awaited our group. This was particularly interesting to me, given the disarmament of civilians following the revolution. Stopping near a large (deactivated) missile, our museum guide casually informed us that symbolically the missile was still pointed north, in the direction of the United States— following the Cuban Missile Crisis—and displayed the government's disdain for America. My jaw dropped. This powerful symbolism stood in extreme juxtaposition to my experience with the Cubans I had met—those who had gotten stars in their eyes when I mentioned America. The government clearly did not speak for those people, and I learned this lesson repeatedly during the following days.

As I had promised myself to interact with as many Cubans

as possible who could answer my questions about what life was like under socialism, I spoke with taxi drivers, waiters, busboys, and hotel staff. I wanted to learn the truth about extreme government interference, and suddenly my world was changed. I received several serious marriage proposals from young Cuban men after I mentioned I was from the United States. They were desperate for an avenue to leave the country and experience their own, in their words, "American dream." They eagerly asked dozens of questions about my life in the United States, and they never forgot to inform me how lucky I was to be an American.

Cubans my age asked what I was studying at my university, and when I responded that I hoped to attend medical school and become a doctor, the stars in their eyes got brighter. Many young Cubans expressed to me their deep desire to become physicians but said it was impossible for them to realize their dreams. I became puzzled by this, as our guide had taught me that education, even medical education, was completely free (other than taxation). The Cubans I interacted with quickly corrected my thinking—yes, it would be "free" for them to attend medical school, but due to the income equity imposed by the government, they could support their families with a substantially higher income working at one of the few *paladares* (non-government-owned restaurants) I mentioned before. It made no financial sense to become a physician. My stomach dropped. Something I had taken for granted so easily in the United States was impossible for so many of my peers in Cuba, simply because of their government's structure.

As I mentioned before, most of our group's scheduled visits were to government-owned and operated facilities. Because we were an American tour group on a specific educational visa, the government had arranged for us to learn everything we could about the "progressive" nature of socialism, which included a stop at Cenesex, the Cuban National Center for Sex Education. This organization is a government-funded body run by Raul Castro's daughter, Mariela, to advance the rights of Cubans in the LGBTQ+ community.[10] While Che Guevara had knowingly imprisoned homosexuals in forced labor camps, Cenesex and Mariela championed the concepts of same-sex marriage and transgender rights. We attended a presentation from a staff member at Cenesex, who gave us the organization's history and informed us of future initiatives. Incredibly, thanks to a revision in the Cuban Constitution, gender identity and sexual orientation were, by then, considered human rights. I was stunned. A nation that fails to honor freedom of speech, imprisons people for speaking out against the government, experiences crumbling infrastructures and food shortages, and fails to inspire its young people to dream of medical school has codified *this* right in its constitution? How did this make any sense?

Every day in the hotel lobby, we discussed and reflected on the day as a school group. Of course, my peers and ethnic studies professors praised almost everything we saw every day, while I was content to sit quietly for the most part. Following our visit to Cenesex, our group reflection was unbearable. Nearly all my classmates spent countless time praising the progressive nature of the Cuban government. They condemned the United States and its system of capitalism for allegedly failing to recognize true equality and

---

10 Emily J. Kirk, "Setting the Agenda for Cuban Sexuality: The Role of Cuba's Cenesex," *Canadian Journal of Latin American and Caribbean Studies* 36, no. 72 (January 2011): 143–63, https://doi.org/10.1080/08263663.2011.10817018.

achieving progressivism, especially for LGBTQ+ Americans, and said that only socialism allows for this equality. Most heartbreakingly, nearly every one of my CSU peers expressed their desire for socialism to replace our freedom in the United States.

I was furious.

My heart raced and my head pounded as I listened to my peers and professors praise the Cuban government, socialism, and one another for condemning American freedom. How could all of them have been so blind to the realities of extreme government control we had quite literally witnessed for days? We had spoken to everyday Cubans, touched the crumbling buildings, sighed at the sight of shirtless children playing soccer in concrete ruins. Ignorance was no longer an excuse. How could they remain *this* blind to the horrors of socialism—the reality of everyone living in equality, but in equality of poverty, misery, and hopelessness?

Toward the end of our trip, we attended a nighttime block party in a small town in Pinar del Rio, a region surrounded by a gorgeous and lush countryside. Block parties are a tradition deeply entangled with the revolution, but they also encourage communities to regularly come together. Words will never be able to describe the depth and width of this experience—an entanglement of cultures, a sadness for the differences in freedom between us, a deep desire to learn about one another, and a bridging of the divide that our governments' political ideologies had created. We applauded performances by local children and musicians, salsa danced with Cuban college students, and held hands with local schoolchildren as we danced and sang the night away.

Again, many young adults who dreamed of going to America approached me and reminded me of my luck. I prayed that my classmates would have a change of heart and open their eyes to the reality in front of them. These Cubans yearned, with every fiber of their being, for true freedom that we Americans often take for granted every day. They told me many stories of people they knew who fled to America in search of a better life—for an opportunity to make their dreams a reality. Like the country itself, the experience was tragically beautiful, and I will never forget the testimonies they shared.

The trip was both frustrating and beautiful all at once. I glimpsed an opposite reality—one without freedom—and I knew I would never again take my American heritage for granted. I had touched, seen, and felt the crushing reality of socialism that breaks the human spirit. I heard Cubans share stories of hopelessness and despair, and I witnessed many beg for a better life, one outside the grip of government control. I never forgot the things I experienced.

As we waited to board our plane back home, we watched as Air Force One landed in Cuba for the first time since 1928. I prayed once more, this time for President Obama, that he would be offered a glimpse into the real Cuba, the one behind the veil the government uses to hide the reality of socialism. I prayed the United States would bring the spark of freedom to the Cuban people who have experienced nothing but socialism yet yearn for an opportunity to build better lives.

After changing planes in Miami, I noticed a newspaper folded neatly into the seatback pocket in front of me. Curious, I picked it up, knowing I had likely missed a substantial number of current events during our trip without much Wi-Fi or cell service. Sprawled across the front page was a story of twenty-seven Cubans who had built a homemade raft out of trash and set sail for the short ninety-mile journey between Havana and Florida, desperately searching for freedom. The day I returned home, a Royal Caribbean cruise ship rescued eighteen of these courageous individuals after twenty-two days at sea. Nine passengers had already perished, and the remaining eighteen were severely dehydrated and malnourished. Though they had made it to the waters off the coast of Southwest Florida, they were taken to the nearest cruise ship port in Cozumel, Mexico.[11] When Cuban refugees fail to set foot on American land, they are repatriated back to Cuba.

Tears began streaming down my face as I finished the story. I had just witnessed the tragedy of socialism, and observing that eighteen unbelievably brave Cubans would return to the misery they fled, likely facing imprisonment or worse, was almost too much to bear. I knew the mainstream media would provide substantial coverage over the next few days of President Obama's historic visit to Cuba, but this story would likely never reach beyond local Miami papers.

Nine refugees paid the ultimate price at sea to avoid continuing a life under socialism. Eighteen others took the same risk, desperate to flee the grip of government overreach. They were all willing to do anything for a life of freedom. How could my classmates, who had witnessed everything I had, have failed to understand that? How could they have

---

11   Carol Rosenberg, "Coast Guard: Nine Cuban Rafters Perish at Sea; 18 Survivors Saved by Cruise Ship," *Miami Herald*, March 19, 2016, https://www.miamiherald.com/news/nation-world/world/americas/cuba/article67043977.html.

still deeply desired the implementation of socialism in the United States?

The thing about the extreme indoctrination happening on American college campuses and in our classrooms is that it's undeniably powerful. For my American classmates, not even seeing the horrors of socialism with their own eyes was enough to change their minds—they remained Che Guevara-T-shirt-wearing, adamant supporters of socialism. Indoctrination is *that* powerful. I will forever understand the importance of educating our nation's next generations with truth, thanks to my experience in Cuba. If we are to prevent socialism from taking hold here in America, we must tell the truth of socialism to empower young Americans to stand up and fight it with that truth.

Today, the intoxication of socialism is spreading throughout America's youth. Seventy percent of millennials (Americans born between 1981 and 1996) say they would vote for a socialist candidate.[12] However, it's clear many Americans don't even understand what socialism is: a 2018 Gallup poll found that only 17 percent of Americans were able to properly define the political system, and 23 percent believe socialism is simply a system of universal equality.[13]

I believe this lack of understanding stems from our nation's college campuses, where young adults are educated to believe the only way to achieve true equality is to institute

---

12   Stef W. Kight, "70 percent of Millennials Say They'd Vote for a Socialist," *Axios*, last modified October 28, 2019, https://www.axios.com/millennials-vote-socialism-capitalism-decline-60c8a6aa-5353-45c4-9191-2de1808dc661.html.

13   Frank Newport, "The Meaning of 'Socialism' to Americans Today," *Gallup*, last modified October 4, 2018, https://news.gallup.com/opinion/polling-matters/243362/meaning-socialism-americans-today.aspx.

complete government control over society within a socialist state. Socialism, however, fails to uphold human rights, advance the human condition, or progress society in any sense. After seeing socialism in action for myself, I know it leads to crushing poverty, destitution, and misery for all but the elite ruling class. It squashes the human spirit and regresses the progress of humanity entirely. Young Americans deserve to be told the truth, on campus and beyond, about socialism: *socialism sucks*.

If you take nothing else away from this book, remember this chapter.

Remember the stories of the young Cubans who yearn for freedom. Remember the crushing equality of misery that those living under socialism are forced to endure. Remember the blindness of my classmates and their unwillingness to see what was right in front of them. If we lose the intellectual battles on our college campuses, if we lose the culture war, if socialism wins, we are headed directly for this harsh reality ourselves.

CHAPTER FOUR

. . . .

A BAD CASE OF THE "-ISMS" AND THE "-OBIAS"

"It doesn't matter if you don't feel oppressed, as a woman in America, you just are. That's the truth of the patriarchy."
—CSU ADMISSIONS OFFICE SUPERVISOR

What's going on inside our nation's college classrooms is unacceptable. An overwhelmingly leftist faculty constantly indoctrinates students with absurd opinions. They academically and/or socially penalize students who fail to oblige them. Truly, however, the most insane intolerance of conservative values and the students who hold them occurs through extracurricular and leadership activities *outside* of the classroom—you know, where the "fun" part of college supposedly occurs. Parents and grandparents often talk about how much fun student government, writing for the campus newspaper, or playing intramural sports were. Usually, those activities alone make adults long for their college days because for them, it was so much *fun*.

Today, however, the fun of college campuses has been all

but sucked away by a politically correct, uptight campus environment too offended by *everything* to have any fun at all. This is particularly true of student leadership positions in extracurricular clubs or organizations—from student government to leadership development programs run by university administrators.

During college orientation, they'll tell you to be open-minded—that college is a place where you can become anyone you want to be. But they don't really mean it. If you choose to be outspoken in your conservative values, I assure you, it is unlikely you will feel fully included in the warm and fuzzy college community. Particularly, to become any sort of formal leader on a college campus (such as a student senator or club president), a working knowledge and practice of social justice are key.

If you've never heard the term "social justice warrior," you're probably not tuned in to the extreme indoctrination occurring on college campuses. Social justice warriors, or SJWs, are self-proclaimed equity activists. Their mission is to expose the "systematic oppression" threatening the success of minorities, women, and students in the LGBTQ+ community. (Don't bother asking SJWs for evidence of this oppression. No explanation will be provided. You'll get stuck in the middle of a temper tantrum.) Students don't come into college with a well-versed understanding of social justice "issues." Instead, the university's culture intentionally and methodically teaches it. High-achieving students are particularly exposed to social justice indoctrination. This is especially true at CSU through the President's Leadership Program (PLP).

PLP is one of many so-called leadership programs on the

CSU campus. It's a multi-year leadership development program for high-achieving incoming college students. Students receive academic credit for participating in and finishing the program in the form of an associate degree in leadership. Admission to the program is highly selective among incoming freshman students, and as of 2021, the program's mission is "To develop active, informed civic leaders who practice ethical, inclusive leadership and embody positive humanitarian characteristics, such as optimism, service to others, passion, mindfulness, and fairness."[14] Sounds like an amazing opportunity, right?

Wrong.

Hiding between the lines of the program's mission is, in fact, a much different goal—to develop the SJWs of the future, committed to ridding universities and our world of "dangerous" conservative ideas and "harmful rhetoric."

While I did not participate in PLP during my time as a student, my sister, who also attended CSU, did throughout her first year. I received a firsthand account of the reality of the program and enthusiastically looked forward to my weekly Tuesday night phone call, where I'd hear the absurd news of each week's class. As it turns out, "informing student leaders" to serve others really means engaging in what I call "Social Justice 101." Each week, students enrolled in PLP complete a required reading assignment pertaining to a particular identity held by a demographic of people—one week focuses on race, another on gender, the next on disability, and so

___

14 "SLiCE Leadership Programs: President's Leadership Program," Colorado State University, accessed September 30, 2020, https://lsc.colostate.edu/slice/slice-leadership/presidents-leadership-program/.

forth. After completing the reading individually, students gather in class once per week to discuss how important each identity is and how people who fall into categories historically perceived as "lesser than" still supposedly need help to compete with the most oppressive beings on planet earth: white, cisgendered, heterosexual males. I shudder just *thinking* about them! (Please sense my sarcasm.)

While my sisters and I may physically seem to be part of an average white family—we're blonde-haired, blue-eyed, and easily sunburned—our extended family has rich cultural traditions from across the world. My mother is the youngest of five children; my father is the youngest of six. So, we have many aunts, uncles, and cousins. My family members have married people from different races, nations, sexual orientations—you name it. My extended family is racially, religiously, ideologically, and in every other way, incredibly diverse. Black, white, Korean, Fijian, Hispanic, Canadian, Native American, transgender, lesbian, heterosexual, Republican, Democrat, Libertarian, Independent, Socialist, redneck, incarcerated, married, divorced, Catholic, Protestant, atheist, and the list goes on and on. For us, these labels have never served to marginalize or create a victim mentality—they have always been a part of being human and what made our family awesome! We were always taught all our family members are equal to one another. We all simply grew up loving one another the way any family would, and we love each other well.

When my sister received the required reading on race relations, she quickly became infuriated. The assigned excerpt, "White Privilege: Unpacking the Invisible Backpack," included statements such as, "I see a pattern running through the matrix of white privilege, a pattern of assumptions that were passed on to me as a white person. There was one main piece of cultural turf; it was my own turf, and I was among those who could control the turf. My skin color was an asset for any move I was educated to want to make."

Here's another quote from the assignment: "Whiteness protected me from many kinds of hostility, distress, and violence, which I was being subtly trained to visit in turn upon people of color." And another, which is perhaps the most horrific, "It seems to me that obliviousness about white advantage, like obliviousness about male advantage, is kept strongly inculturated in the United States so as to maintain the myth of meritocracy. The myth that democratic choice is equally available to all."

My sister and I (indeed, our entire family) know that all members of our family, regardless of what they look like, have always experienced a better and more prosperous life than the generation before them, thanks to their parents' hard work and the American system. My sister knew this article was anything but true. Amidst her frustration, she researched dozens of evidence-based publications and articles that put her singular, biased, assigned reading to shame. She had not yet been vocal about her political beliefs in class, yet, she knew it was time to either share the truth with her classmates or run the risk they would never hear the truth at all.

Immediately after her next class began, her instructor asked for the students' response to the weekly reading. When no one else raised their hand, my sister bravely exclaimed the two powerful words that would change the course of her semester: "I disagree." She went on to share peer-reviewed Harvard studies disproving the concept that being black made someone predisposed to police brutality, evidence-based articles disproving a race gap in higher education, and more. Both her peers and instructors were floored. It was as if they had never even heard a conservative opinion, let alone experienced a student disagreeing with a single assignment in the class—*ever*.

As it turns out, it is highly likely the instructors and directors of PLP had never experienced a student vocally disagreeing. Typically, over half the students in the program drop out after the first semester; they do it quietly, so they don't cause any harm to their reputation with the faculty. But now, the instructors were faced with a unique situation—a student who did *not* plan on quitting but who was willing to vocalize her dissent. They were shook. They postponed the entire curriculum for the next week's module to create a "safe conversation space" in response to some "dangerous ideas" that had been proposed during class. (Dangerous ideas? Seriously?!) The concept that all people are created equal and should be treated as such in the United States is now considered a *dangerous idea*?

Let that sink in.

The instructor herself shared that she was "visibly upset" upon returning home after class and was "crying with her partner" over the hatred uttered by my sister. Other students claimed they felt "unsafe" in a room with my sister's "oppressive" commentary and that racism was alive and well on our campus.

If I didn't know my sister, maybe I'd buy into this narrative. Most students sitting around her gawked in dismay at the instructor's slanderous accusations—my sister is the type of person who would never harm a bug, let alone another human being, and despite political disagreement, her peers knew this to be true. In no way is my sister combative: she is a giving and loving person to everyone. She has no hidden agenda of racism, and to insinuate she was somehow a dangerous person spewing hateful rhetoric is comical. She simply shared with her classmates her belief that all people are equal. She simply encouraged thoughtful dialogue. (Since when does *that* make you an evil person?)

Yet, leftist faculty and administrative members are so terrified of conservative ideas that they won't hesitate to slanderously label a conservative student to keep them from speaking up. So, my sister's speech was labeled as hateful, oppressive, and unsafe. I would be surprised, except, by that point, I had experienced many of the same situations as a senior at CSU. Watching my younger sister undergo many moments of political frustration in her classes was expected.

Outside of PLP, I had many parallel experiences in multiple leadership positions. I have always been a naturally inclined leader; throughout my life, I've strived to serve through positions of leadership, from speech and debate captain (and competing at the national debate tournament twice in high school) to representing Colorado at the annual Distinguished Young Women scholarship program in 2015. My tendency toward leadership continued into college, where I fell in love with how many unique organizations and activities existed at CSU, a large, public university. I wouldn't trade many of the experiences I had there for the world—I was a caretaker for our live mascot (CAM the Ram), played intramural sports, and was involved with my local church community. Other roles were trying, like my student employee job as an admissions ambassador during my freshman and sophomore years.

As an admissions ambassador, I was tasked with providing tours to prospective students and their families, calling admitted students to answer questions, working the admissions office front desk, and speaking on panels for high school students and their families during campus visit days.

The ambassador team was selected from a massive pool of applicants through a series of individual and group interviews designed to understand the unique strengths each ambassador could bring to the team. After making the cut, I was shocked that I was one of a handful of Christians or conservatives on the team. Most of the student team, handpicked to represent our massive student body of over 33,000 students, studied ethnic or gender studies, were activists of reproductive or environmental justice organizations, or were undocumented, illegal students. It seemed the most important criteria for selecting student ambassadors was not that each candidate had experience in public speaking or giving tours or even being personable in an interview, but rather that they had a unique (and very leftist) quality about them that the admissions office could use to fulfill some checkbox on the list of diverse identities.

Much to my dismay, as admissions ambassadors, we were required to attend frequent social justice training seminars where we learned how to become a more "welcoming" office to those of diverse identities (unless, of course, those identities happened to fall into the Christian or conservative realm). Often, we discussed topics such as "checking your privilege," introducing yourself with appropriate gender pronouns, and avoiding "triggering" phrases on campus tours, so as not to offend prospective students or their parents.

The most absurd of these meetings occurred just before the election of President Trump, during which each ambassador was given a coloring page of eyeglasses. Inside the lenses of the glasses, the faculty staff instructed us to write our identities, which supposedly make up the "lens" through which we view the world. Our identities included race, gender, sexual orientation, religious preference, socioeconomic status, etc.

My pair of glasses looked a bit like this:

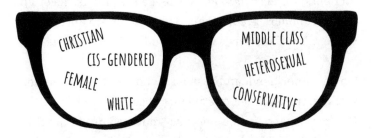

When most other students filled out their glasses, they included words like this:

As a freshman, I hadn't yet been often exposed to leftist or social justice indoctrination. So, I assumed my pair of glasses was acceptable. After all, I have no control over what socioeconomic class, race, or family I was born into—it simply happened to occur by God's plan. While I can control my religious and political affiliations, I had never been told that it was "evil" to believe in Jesus Christ or that it was "immoral" to check the "R" box on my voter registration.

Boy, oh, boy (pardon the "gendered" phrase), was I wrong.

The faculty reprimanded the few students whose glasses resembled mine for possessing and publicly noting the identities over which we had no control. "Check your privilege," they told us when encountering coworkers or prospective students; we needed to acknowledge that life is easier and the world offers greater opportunities for advancement to white, Christian, conservative, middle-class students.

On the other hand, ambassadors who identified as undocumented, transgender, or students of color were heralded as the heroes who walk among us—not because of anything these students *did*, but rather because of the identities they held. According to the faculty, because some had more melanin in their skin or were attracted to the same sex, they would undoubtedly be unsuccessful in most of their endeavors. This, of course, was the fault of students whose glasses looked like mine. (Let the indoctrination process accelerate.)

During the discussion, one student employee asked our supervisor why being female meant she was at a disadvantage. After all, she noted, she was a student in the engineering program—which was overwhelmingly male—and she had faced no obstacles academically or professionally, consistently ranked as a top student in her courses, and had received student employment offers in her field. Sensing the slightest dissent to the point of the activity, our boss rapidly interrupted the student's question, explaining it didn't matter if she had *felt* any oppression as a female engineer, the oppression nonetheless *existed*, but she was simply too naïve to recognize its ever-crushing weight on her life.

My colleague was swiftly rebuked and discredited by the "real professionals" in the room—our supervisors—as soon as she expressed any doubt that her experience as a young woman in the sciences on today's college campuses was anything but equitable. The point of this exercise became immediately clear. This wasn't about diversity, which would ideally lead to unity. Rather, it was our employer's thinly veiled threat. The message was apparent: "You must agree, or else."

Later in the semester, I met more leftist bureaucracy—this time, with consequences. Per our training, the admissions ambassadors were to never, *ever*, utter the phrase "you guys" when referencing tour groups or coworkers; this is, apparently, a "gendered" term excluding (and therefore oppressing) females and "other genders" who do not identify as male. Supposedly, "you guys" furthers collegiate patriarchy—something I have never experienced. Uttering the two words side by side would result in a consequential diatribe from our supervisors, who were both female! (Some patriarchy, huh?)

Being from Colorado, cutting the phrase from my vocabulary was a difficult task—it is akin to asking someone from Texas or Alabama to stop saying "y'all." "You guys" is simply a term Coloradans use to grab the attention of an entire group. I had used the phrase since I could talk and had never been told it was offensive. Even as a woman, I had never noticed the supposed "gendered language" of this phrase. Rather, when I am included in the expression, I feel included.

However, I would soon learn that the political-correctness police ruled in the admissions office after I used the phrase with a tour group gearing up for a campus visit.

A fellow admissions ambassador overheard me utter the forbidden phrase and reported my mistake to our supervisor, who issued a formal reprimand, placing a note in my file as a warning. She was required to document my shortcomings in case any future dismissal from my job were to be warranted. All this for two simple, nonthreatening words, which likely were not offensive to a single individual on that tour.

These two experiences—drawing my "privilege glasses" and receiving a formal reprimand for saying "you guys"—signaled the leftist indoctrination I would experience throughout my undergraduate career. They solidified an important lesson: college is often more focused on indoctrination than education, ensuring that students adopt a passionate belief in everything authority figures on campus promote, rather than questioning perspectives.

I would discover that universities are stubbornly determined to fundamentally change the way students understand diversity. At universities, diversity is no longer a concept that celebrates the differences among individuals to establish common ground. Instead, diversity programs and initiatives on college campuses are meant to divide students by ranking the importance of each individual based on how many "oppressed" identities they carry. I would eventually understand that conservative students had little to no representation among student leadership positions on campus or in the admissions office—and all along the way, faculty, staff, and sometimes other students encourage them to remain quiet and comply at all costs.

This carefully cultivated culture of leftism in extracurricular activities sends a clear message to conservative students—comply, or else. Students with a conservative mindset must embrace the Left's doctrine of diversity or risk feeling out of place and unwelcome. As I had discovered, if a student dares to push the boundaries of the lockstep culture of leftism, they may find themselves dealing with disciplinary actions that remain documented on their permanent school record.

This is not just about the *classroom;* conservative ideas are typically unwelcome among student *activities*, even beyond academics. I know, because leftism wasn't done with me yet.

Little did I know, I would soon experience the full extent of extremism in one of the most leftist organizations on campus: student government.

. . . .

CHAPTER FIVE

STUDENT GOVERNMENT OR PARTISAN POLITICS?

"Because you have blonde hair and blue eyes, your experience doesn't matter. You enjoy privileges and opportunities people of color don't have for themselves."

—CSU STUDENT SENATOR, 2017

Working for the CSU admissions office submerged me directly into the heart of leftist indoctrination on campus, indicative of colleges' overall unwelcoming culture toward conservatives. One position completely altered my college experience: student government.

During high school, I competed in student congress, in which students act as members of Congress and debate mock legislation. I fell in love with parliamentary procedure and the legislative process. Naturally, then, I wanted to be a student senator for my college in the Associated Students of Colorado State University (ASCSU)—CSU's student government.

Just before I was elected, the organization had ended the

previous semester by passing an incredibly controversial piece of legislation known as the "Diversity Bill," fundamentally changing the structure of our student senate. Previously, senators represented their individual academic colleges, such as the College of Business or the College of Liberal Arts. Each college received a certain number of seats depending on their student body size; each college then individually voted on their own representatives from their college to fill those seats.

But the Diversity Bill created several new senator seats, one for each of CSU's Student Diversity Programs and Services (SDPS) offices, each of which represented a particular demographic, from the Black and African American Cultural Center to the Women's and Gender Advocacy Center. The bill proposed these students would *not* be elected from their peers within the student body but rather would be *chosen* by the faculty directors of each office they represented. Here's why this matters: student senators are primarily responsible for voting on bills and resolutions that decide how student fees are allocated. Student fees are non-optional fees that students must pay, along with tuition, to the university. ASCSU oversees the entire annual budget of student fees, which they allocate to student public transportation, health center, recreation center, programming and speaker opportunities, the salaries of student government members, hosting diversity symposiums and conferences, and more. For instance, if a club wants to host a speaker who charges a $15,000 speaker fee, they ask the Student Fee Review Board in ASCSU for a grant, which is later approved by the student senate according to the bylaws. This process often leads to a lopsided allotment of funds to leftist organizations on college campuses, given the uneven ratio of leftist to conservative voices in student government associations.

Generally, the annual student fee budget at CSU is around $60 million, a significant figure by any measure.

This bill created a substantial block of voting student senators who would not be accountable to the students whose money they were allocating; instead, these senators would be chosen by leftist faculty members. Essentially, this was a massive step toward funding leftism by the millions.

A handful of student senators, conservative and liberal alike, vehemently opposed the legislation because the proposed new senators would not be elected by their peers but would instead be accountable to the faculty. Moreover, opposing senators further argued that not every demographic on campus would be represented, as the SDPS offices failed to represent a key set of identities—religious affiliations. When opposing senators suggested the Diversity Bill not pass and cast their votes accordingly, all hell broke loose. The Diversity Bill vote happened the same evening I attended orientation to run for student senate, so I was in the room where it happened.

So many people showed to witness and voice their support or dissent for the controversial legislation that the senate meeting, ordinarily held in the designated senate chambers, was relocated to a ballroom with a 1,500-person seating capacity to allow for a larger audience. Priests and rabbis from the community, as well as employees and a wide variety of students, shared their opinions during open discussion—which, that evening, lasted more than three hours.

Ultimately, the legislation passed, but not before the faculty, staff, and student body viciously denounced the student senators who voted against it as racists, white supremacists, Nazis, and the like. This was especially ironic considering most of those who voted "no" held minority identities themselves—Hispanic, Jewish, female, or otherwise.

I was taken aback.

I was still a freshman, and I was reluctant to engage in the conversation, fearing being labeled such terrible things. Still, I ran for a position in our student senate anyway. The race started in March, just after spring break, and students voted online and on campus. I won my race, securing a senate seat for the College of Veterinary Medicine and Biomedical Sciences. So, come May, I showed up to a now-packed senate chamber that included several new SDPS senators.

Despite the newfound ASCSU controversy, I was ecstatic.

Student government offered various professional development opportunities, so I dove headfirst into every single one. I joined the Senate Leadership Team as the Director of Outreach, working to engage with our campus community. I wrote and sponsored several pieces of legislation seeking to improve the student experience. I joined committees to hash out ideas to serve the student body in meaningful ways. Yet, I kept my head down during times of controversy, and for months, I refused to give the overwhelmingly leftist group of my peers any ammunition to use against me and my politics.

That is, until I snapped.

As I mentioned, the student government has the ultimate say on student fee matters, including fee allocation and how much to charge students in the first place. Wielding so much fiscal responsibility often gives student senators quite the feeling of power, and they frequently pass (nonbinding) legislation called resolutions to express their opinion to the university administration. Other times, the student government creates more lighthearted (again, nonbinding) legislation like Resolution 4607, which congratulated our student newspaper on 125 years of "distinguished service." Mostly, these student government resolutions are arbitrary, congratulating students or organizations on achievements or celebrating holidays. But sometimes, these resolutions get purely political—and that's when it gets ugly.

When Resolution 4613—Solidarity with the Standing Rock Sioux Tribe—was proposed for the first time in my elected term, I understood why the Diversity Bill had been so controversial.

Resolution 4613 concerned the North Dakota protests over the Dakota Access Pipeline and the native Sioux tribe whose land was to be affected by the construction of the pipeline. At the time, the pipeline was one of the most controversial political topics leading up to the 2016 presidential election. In such a predominately left-wing group as the ASCSU legislature, a warm and fuzzy resolution like this one, designed to support our students' right to travel to North Dakota and protest alongside members of the Sioux tribe, was to be expected.

At first, I didn't even see a problem with the legislation—as a conservative, I will fight until my dying breath for the right to free speech for everyone, even if I personally disagree with those protesting. Once I began reading the legislation, however, I found a clause that completely changed my opinion of it.

> "THEREFORE BE IT HEREBY FURTHER RESOLVED that the 46th Senate of the Associated Students of Colorado State University recognizes that the United States Army Corps of Engineers took the proper considerations into account when deciding to not issue a permit for the current path of the pipeline."

Suddenly, this warm and fuzzy resolution designed to promote the First Amendment turned into a declaration of opinion *about* the pipeline and, therefore, was politically motivated speech itself. Apparently, the student government was going to directly declare the political opinion of all 33,000 students attending CSU. I knew that at least one of those 33,000 students disagreed with this statement: me. Statistically, there had to be hundreds, if not thousands, of others on campus who felt the same. So, I believed it was immoral for our legislative body to make such a declaration, knowing that varying political opinions existed on our campus.

I calmly raised this concern during discussion and debate by asking why it was our responsibility to consider the legislation in the first place. I brought up the Native American history within my own family. (My great-grandmother was part of the Cherokee Tribe in Oklahoma, so Native American history and culture have always been an important facet of our family tradition.) I shared that there may even be students with ties to the Native American culture who may support the construction of the Dakota Access pipeline, and it was not the responsibility of our student legislature to tell them they're "wrong" for holding such a belief.

You'd have thought the sky was falling.

Just raising a simple question incited extreme chaos.

At first, I was quietly pulled aside by the SDPS diversity senators and told I had offended many people on our campus and in the SDPS offices for sharing my Native American history because of my white skin, blonde hair, and blue eyes. It didn't matter that my family history was true—all that mattered was what I looked like on the outside—and because I didn't possess traditional features of a Native American, it "didn't count." (Maybe someone should tell them that Senator Elizabeth Warren's 1/1024 genetic makeup of Native American "doesn't count.") I was told that even if I didn't mean to do it, I was suppressing minority communities on our campus and injecting hateful, "supremacist" dialogue into our student body.

I was later informed that a few of the SDPS offices even put photos of me on the walls so that students involved in their leadership would know exactly who to discuss problematic language with. One student senator, who at the time represented the Black/African American Cultural Center, calmly told me, "It wouldn't matter if you were half-black. Because you look like *this* (gesturing to my body), you enjoy privileges and opportunities people of color don't have for themselves."

Are you kidding me? Since when is judging people solely by the color of their skin acceptable? Last time I checked, passing judgment on someone or their opinions based solely on the amount of melanin in their skin is called one thing: *racism*.

This was the first time I had ever been blatantly referred to as racist—and it stung. *Really* stung. I ran home from the senate meeting and cried. A dark cloud hung over me for a week, causing me to anxiously wonder how I had said or done anything to lead anyone to believe I held any racist viewpoints. I was crushed, but I knew that passing legislation defining certain political positions as universally held within our student body was wrong, so I forged ahead.

After the quiet conversations solicited by leftist senators and faculty members failed to silence my opposition to the resolution, the Left's tactics in our student legislature became significantly more obvious and aggressive. I was directly referred to as a racist by many of my colleagues on the senate floor, in front of fellow students, faculty members, and administrative officials, and no one batted an eye. As soon as I attempted to defend myself, however, I was quickly silenced by the loud pounding of the gavel held by the vice president under the guise of "maintaining decorum."

In that moment, I snapped, and I just *got it*.

Suddenly, everything about my college campus made perfect sense to me. I wasn't surprised that these students honestly believed I was a racist simply because I held conservative viewpoints—that's what they had been taught from the first moment they set foot on campus. It was incredibly likely that every administrator, faculty member, professor, graduate teaching assistant, and even resident assistant (RA) they had ever encountered was firmly planted with their roots growing deep, far on the left side of the aisle. Many of my peers hadn't grown up discussing various viewpoints in politics with their families the way I had, and perhaps they had no political foundation on which to base their views of the world before attending college. Thus, they simply took everything their professors and faculty members had to say as fact, rather than opinion, and I was sick and tired of it. (By the way, the resolution passed, but not without first removing the clause stating the senate body's support for ending the pipeline project. My resistance paid off.)

Leftists in student government are fantastic at spreading rhetoric that helps their cause, until the opposition shows up. When that happens, they will typically back down. From that day forward, I used my voice on campus, regardless of the fact that my conservative and Christian upbringing would likely offend many of my peers and nearly all my professors. I was no longer afraid of the consequences. I knew the worst thing the Left could do was slander me as a racist, white supremacist, or Nazi. Truthfully, the first time someone calls you a racist, it hurts. A lot. It might even hurt for the first dozen or two dozen times. Eventually, however, I realized when someone chose to call me something so vile and so baseless, they had nothing else to call me out on, no facts to offer. Typically, this was a clear sign that I was doing something right, that I was moving the needle and changing the tide of opinion on my campus.

I had finally "come out" as a conservative.

My secret identity was out there among my peers, and they discovered there was an elusive conservative student among them. I'd later discover there were many, but they lacked a trailblazer.

Being called a racist for opposing that resolution was the first of infinite labels I would soon have assigned to me. Through my journey with various student leadership positions, particularly student government, I discovered campuses have a bad case of the "-isms" and "-obias." Others, with nothing better to argue, try to silence conservative students, faculty members, and visiting speakers by categorizing them and their beliefs under racism, sexism, misogynism, homophobia, islamophobia, transphobia, white supremacy, and other big words. (What a mouthful!)

The whole system succeeds as long as conservatives remain afraid of receiving any of these horrible labels. For most, this threat is enough to silence them for their entire college experience, and perhaps even beyond. Even worse, I've witnessed deeply convicted conservatives and even Christians walk away from and abandon their fundamental values and embrace radical leftism out of fear of receiving one of these labels. On the flip side, leftists throw out these words and labels like candy. If anyone possesses the slightest tinge of conservative thought, the Left casts them aside as hateful, racist, misogynist, homophobic, transphobic, or any combination of the laundry list of insults commonly uttered by your typical campus SJW. It's heartbreaking, and it's happening now, as you read these words, on practically every college campus in America.

My interactions with this hostile, far-left environment continued far beyond the passage of the Dakota Access Pipeline resolution. Later in my student government career, and after

I had outwardly proclaimed to be a conservative student on campus, I was approached by a nonpartisan, nationwide student-led coalition known as Students for Opioid Solutions, who paved the way to end opioid overdoses among students on college campuses. As a Biomedical Sciences student, working to advance policy that would benefit the health of students on my campus was a dream come true. Together, this group and I drafted legislation for ASCSU that would advocate for RAs to carry and be trained to use the lifesaving drug for overdose situations—naloxone.

Naloxone, often referred to as Narcan, is an emergency drug administered to someone who is suffering from an opioid overdose. It could not be easier to administer, particularly in its common form of a nasal spray. The side effects are also minimal; even if Narcan is administered to someone who is sober, there is only a 0.2 percent chance of nausea and/or dizziness, and more severe side effects, such as seizures, are even less likely.[15] Anyone can safely administer Narcan and save someone's life within minutes. Simply put, it can be a miracle drug, and it's often the last opportunity to save someone's life.

In 2018, when the Students for Opioid Solutions approached me about the legislation, the national movement to train and equip civilians on carrying and administering naloxone had taken off—public libraries, high schools, and other community organizations were implementing similar policies.

---

15 Donald M. Yealy, et. al., "The Safety of Prehospital Naloxone Administration by Paramedics," *Annals of Emergency Medicine* 19, no. 8 (August 1990): 902–5, https://doi.org/10.1016/s0196-0644(05)81566-5; Daniel P. Wermeling, "Review of Naloxone Safety for Opioid Overdose: Practical Considerations for New Technology and Expanded Public Access," *Therapeutic Advances in Drug Safety* 6, no. 1 (January 26, 2015): 20–31, https://doi.org/10.1177/2042098614564776.

Because of these resounding facts, it's no wonder Resolution 4715: Declaration of Support for the Saving of Lives and the Prevention of Opioid Overdoses on the Campus of CSU passed unanimously within the ASCSU Senate. Even the most far-left student senators who had, until then, vehemently opposed any legislation with my name on it approached me following the resolution's passage, thanking and praising me for implementing real solutions for real student problems. We unified to fulfill our oath to serve students.

The resolution was nonbinding and needed faculty and administrative support to be enacted. To gain their approval, I wanted to show as broad support across campus as possible, so I drafted the resolution with the Residence Hall Association (RHA), which is essentially the university's student government for RA's and other residence life student leadership, making it the first-ever joint resolution between the ASCSU and RHA.

I had discussed the resolution in detail with the then-president of RHA. She assured me the RHA senators would approve of the programming. After the resolution passed, I proudly (and, in hindsight, naively) presented the legislation to RHA, which seemed to be going wonderfully, at first— until I suddenly found myself in the midst of yet another ideological battle over how to best aid millions of Americans who may struggle with opioid addiction (a few of whom were likely students on our campus).

At first, RHA senators tried to strategically maneuver away from their real hesitation with the bill by claiming that it was illegal for RAs to even touch a student dealing with an overdose. I knew this was false—Colorado is one of many states which had implemented a "Good Samaritan Law," which legally protects civilians from potential litigation if they come to another's aid in a medical emergency. Soon, however, I discovered the underlying reason for RHA's blatant repudiation of the legislation. It all boiled down to identity politics.

I had completed thorough research on opioid abuse and addiction. I had included several vital statistics regarding the rapidly growing opioid crisis in the contents of the resolution itself (which have now become grossly outdated with the accelerated spread of opioid abuse nationwide). I included research that suggested drug overdoses and alcohol abuse often are rarely reported on college campuses to prevent negative publicity for the university. Shockingly, however, my peers were unwilling to acknowledge any data or statistical evidence. Why? According to the hardheaded RHA senators, the opioid crisis was a "white" and "declining" issue.

Yes, you read that right.

Apparently, prescription drug and opioid abuse, which in 2017 alone killed more than 70,000 Americans—more Americans killed than by guns, car crashes, or HIV/AIDS in any single year and more even than the death toll from the Vietnam and Iraq Wars *combined*[16]—was another "white" problem that was unworthy of consideration. One RHA senator stated on the floor, "I find it disheartening that ASCSU has failed bills in the past that support minorities but were quick to pass this issue that primarily affects the

---

16 "Overdose Death Rates," National Institute on Drug Abuse, last modified March 10, 2020, https://www.drugabuse.gov/drug-topics/trends-statistics/overdose-death-rates.

white population," conflating saving student lives with a racist, supremacist agenda. Other students claimed that the nationwide opioid crisis was "declining" in its effects and wouldn't continue to kill Americans at breakneck speed. (Boy, were they wrong. The annual death toll increased from 50,000 Americans in 2015, to 65,000 Americans in 2016, to 70,000 Americans in 2017. It wasn't declining. It was accelerating.[17]).

I couldn't believe this nonsense. The opioid crisis had recently graced the pages of nearly every major newspaper and had been frequently mentioned on virtually every major news network nationwide. It had become a national topic of conversation and was affecting every demographic. The opioid crisis had not discriminated against any socio-economic status, age, geography, or race—so why was RHA choosing to do so?

To this day, I cannot understand why the legislation failed in the RHA senate; it makes no sense. Moreover, the suggestion that anyone combatting the opioid crisis is a blatant racist, committed to a problem that "primarily affects the white population," was truly one of the most disgusting lies I encountered in college. To the Left, since a conservative student senator wrote the legislation, it must be tainted with white supremacy. The "-isms" and "-obias" were present in full force once again, and they clearly weren't going anywhere.

I refused to let these labels and the possibility of leftist backlash prevent me from holding leadership positions. After my

---

17 Ibid.

tumultuous experience as a student senator and particularly after being called a racist on the senate floor, I decided to enact true protection for the speech of all student senators. So, in 2017, my sophomore year, while still a senator, I ran for a brand-new position in ASCSU—Speaker of the Senate, and I won with a 400+ majority (typically, student body presidents only won by a few dozen votes).

I was suddenly the third-highest ranking member of our student government, which meant my calendar filled up with multiple weekly meetings with faculty and administration from across the university. While serving as Speaker, I received an inside look into how our nation's public universities operate from the administration level down.

I met regularly with university administrators to share what was on the student legislative agenda. I quickly discovered that, outside of the handful of students within leadership positions, our administrators were largely out of touch with the student body. They only heard feedback from the student government and student organization leaders, a handful of students who, for the most part, all thought the same way. I soon learned most faculty committees and administrative councils (such as the Commission on Women and Gender Equity or even the Board of Governors for the University) had little or no student voice presence at all, despite the fact students are the reason a university exists in the first place.

I also began to understand the personal perspectives of the faculty and staff. I soon discovered that, often, two factors drive leftist university administrators—power and fear. Typically, those whose jobs are centered around diversity and inclusion efforts are driven by power. They understand they can use their position as a tenured administrator to influence the campus dynamic—from hosting diversity conferences and events to determining what words or phrases are banned from campus (like "long time no see," which I mentioned earlier). On the flip side, other administrators, even high-ranking ones, are often driven by fear. Even some of the good-hearted people I discussed in the introduction, those who wish to be more evenhanded, are afraid of the adverse consequences that stem from standing up to the Left.

These ideologically diverse members of the university administration and faculty *are* present on campus. (I know because many of them have spoken to me.) Like the students, however, they conform to the wave of socialist ideology and social justice training, if only to keep their jobs. Often, these administrators are so afraid of offending people, they will destroy themselves for every leftist cause but fail to help conservative students. As a student employee, I was required to spend many hours focusing on how to make our university more inclusive to social justice causes, how our administration could fight more for diversity, and how we could rid our campus of "hatred" (more commonly known as "conservative thought"). Yet, often, these efforts actually exclude conservatives and don't make students feel equal.

My personal experiences have led me to understand that often, leadership positions on campus are only sustainable for a certain type of student—a leftist. Similarly, diversity-oriented administrators, offices, and programs like the SDPS offices at CSU, the PLP program, and our Vice President for Diversity, are vital to propagating leftist indoctrination. In fact, none of these entities would even exist if students weren't pitted against one another. So, leftist students are given a multitude of "leadership positions" in college where they are taught to believe that most students are at a disadvantage to conservative students on their campus, and the cycle continues.

For example, the director of the Black/African American Cultural Center at CSU would be out of a job if the black students on campus were encouraged to believe that they can succeed the same as white students. At CSU alone, dozens of faculty members, administrative officials, and professors have jobs that center on diversity initiatives—but I question if they really want to "fix" the supposed problems of division on our campus. If there were no longer any problems, their jobs would no longer exist! Thus, these individuals have a personal stake in bringing cultural differences to light in a stirring and emotionally driven way, pitting students against one another. After all, perceived or real, division among students fuels the need for their positions and resulting paychecks.

While my unique position as Speaker offered a holistic understanding of the student body, my student government experiences were not isolated instances; student government organizations are among the most aggressive and combative entities toward conservative students, and they also have the worst case of the "-isms" and "-obias."

* * *

In 2018, Isabella Chow, who's both an Asian and a Christian, made headlines as a student senator at UC Berkeley. She refused to support a student government resolution that disavowed Trump's failure to include a legal definition of gender in his Title IX changes. Allegedly, this omission leaves those who identify with neither gender subject to discrimination.[18] Isabella cited her Christian faith as her basis of opposing the resolution, saying, "At the end of the day, I believe in objective truth." Fellow senators arrived at the following legislative sessions protesting with massive banners that said, "Senator Chow Resign Now." Isabella refused to engage in the angry banter, determined to demonstrate how the Christian community can show love to even those with whom they disagree. "As a Christian, I believe that God redeems, and he uses all situations for the good of those who love Him. There is so much happening, and even though it's been a really, really rough week for me, I know that God is working, and I know that he is using this to strengthen the church, to awaken the church in a sense," she shared in an interview with *Campus Reform*.

Isabella quickly became a direct target of UC Berkeley's "-isms" and "-obias"—and it affected her campus experience far beyond student government. She later shared with the *San Francisco Chronicle*, "I go to classes, and people are looking at me. I've been painted in such a negative light. Everybody's talking about it. No matter how much I tried to say, 'I can love you and still disagree with you,' people still interpret my disagreement with being a bigot and a hater."[19] (I later had the wonderful privilege of interviewing

---

18 Nanette Asimov, "UC Berkeley campus senator abstains from a vote. Now students want her out," *San Francisco Chronicle*, last modified November 9, 2018, https://www.sfchronicle.com/bayarea/article/UC-Berkeley-campus-senator-abstains-from-a-vote-13378621.php#photo-16472734.

19 Celine Ryan, "Berkeley Student Senator Disavowed over Christian Beliefs Responds to Calls to RESIGN," *Campus Reform*, last modified November 8, 2018, https://www.campusreform.org/?ID=11505.

Isabella for my video series, *On The Front Lines*, following my graduation from CSU.)

This destructive behavior tends to spread beyond student government, often escalating into full-blown violence. In February 2019, Hayden Williams, a conservative activist for the Leadership Institute, was tabling on the UC Berkeley campus recruiting students to the organization when he was repeatedly shoved and eventually punched in the face by Zachary Greenberg.[20] The local police department took many days to respond and failed to arrest the suspect for nearly two weeks following the attack. Conservative students nationwide were outraged by the lack of response, and many prominent conservative figures, including Donald Trump, Jr., used social media to share the clear leftist bias that often puts conservative students in harm's way on college campuses.

Amazingly, outbursts from leftists on our campuses are not always verbal—they are progressively becoming more violent, leaving behind black eyes and broken skin.

Stories like Hayden's and Isabella's are heartbreaking and numerous, but don't get me wrong—I firmly encourage conservative students to get as involved as possible on their campuses. Given my own family background and upbringing, I also wholeheartedly agree with the (supposed) intentions underlying diversity initiatives—we *should* all be celebrating our identity as one community, despite our inward and

---

20 Katie Mettler, "Police Have Arrested the Man They Say Punched a Conservative Activist at UC Berkeley," *The Washington Post*, last modified March 1, 2019, https://www. washingtonpost.com/education/2019/02/27/conservative-activist-was-punched-face-uc-berkeley-response-enraged-right/?noredirect=on&utm_term=.1691f85a95dd.

outward differences. However, my idea of diversity includes diversity of thought in addition to that of immutable characteristics.

Throughout my leadership experiences at CSU, I learned more about myself and what it truly means to be a strong leader—particularly to those who disagree with me—than I have learned through anything else in my adult life. For the most part, however, leadership positions on today's college campuses are shallow façades for social justice and diversity initiatives. Known conservative students are typically at a disadvantage to receive one of these positions and are often driven out of them altogether. This clever ruse remains the big secret that the world outside of campus life doesn't know about. Once I discovered this truth for myself, I knew something had to change at CSU. It was time to speak up—to fully come out as a conservative—outside of the four walls of the student government office. It was time for a turning point.

CHAPTER SIX

. . . .

MY TURNING POINT

"There will be no safe spaces or trigger warnings here. We encourage you to challenge what you believe and why you believe it."
—CHARLIE KIRK, YWLS OPENING SESSION 2017

During ASCSU's Dakota Access Pipeline Resolution, I snapped—on the student senate floor and in my own life. I had been relentlessly referred to as a racist in student government, had lost nearly all my friends after I voiced my support for President Trump, and I felt incredibly isolated from my peers as "that conservative girl" on campus. Yet strangely, I somehow felt more empowered than ever before, especially to serve as an advocate for conservatism at my college.

The Left is very skilled at ensuring conservative students feel isolated. Often, I felt as if I were the lone conservative in a sea of 33,000 students, without a place to call my own. Logically, I knew this couldn't be true, but I had no idea what I could do to make a change, bridging the divide between myself and other conservatives around me—that is, until April of my sophomore year.

In the Spring of 2017, I was sitting in the ASCSU office with my headphones on, completing my weekly senatorial duties, preparing for my new position as the Speaker, and doing everything I could to avoid interacting with the unforgiving leftist students (who, at this point, were my own personal anti-fan club). Truthfully, I wasn't working on anything in particular, but I didn't want to stop using my computer and give my peers time to confront me. I started aimlessly scrolling through Facebook, and a bright pink and purple advertisement glossed with the faces of Carly Fiorina, Ben Shapiro, and Tomi Lahren caught my eye. I had followed Carly's presidential campaign closely in 2016, and I had recently started watching videos of Ben Shapiro speaking on college campuses and of Tomi's "Final Thoughts" videos. Impulsively, I clicked. I landed on an eye-catching website advertising a conference in Dallas for conservative high school and college females, which I later came to know and love as Turning Point USA's annual Young Women's Leadership Summit (YWLS). Something compelled me to apply, although I had little familiarity with most of the conference speakers, and I certainly didn't know what Turning Point USA was. But after submitting an application and booking a flight, it was settled.

I would be heading to YWLS in a few months.

Before I hopped on a plane to Texas, I headed east to Washington, DC to represent ASCSU and CSU at another annual collegiate women's conference, hosted by a prominent leftist organization: the American Association of Undergraduate Women (AAUW). A high-ranking member of the CSU administration had financially sponsored my attendance at the conference through university funding, hoping it would empower me as a female leader. Throughout the entire conference, however, I felt anything *but* empowered.

AAUW's conference, boasting a massive attendance of over eight hundred female college leaders, began with an immediate separation of ideology. The hosts took the stage and began explaining the opening activity: the emcee would read a series of statements, and then the young women would identify themselves by standing to show their agreement or disagreement with the various statements, including "I feel that society puts me at a lesser place than males," "I feel oppressed when I adorn my identities and step into the world every day," and "I am ashamed of our nation's president, Donald Trump." Less than five percent of the room stood up in opposition to those statements, and here's the kicker—the moderators of the conference walked around with a microphone, asking you to identify why you stood for what you believed. In doing so, they immediately pointed a metaphorical finger at the small number of conservatives in the room, as if to say, "Don't associate with *those* girls." Knowing no one at the conference, it was terrifying to stand virtually alone in defense of my values. Although I did so, I was isolated from most attendees at the conference. For a leadership conference, I sure didn't feel surrounded by leaders. I felt surrounded by bullies.

The next few days were full of leftist statements and values, as if it would be impossible for a young woman in student leadership to be a conservative. Nearly every session began with the ever-present "trigger warning"—a preemptive warning something a speaker or moderator was yet to say may potentially offend someone in the room—and the young women around me would instinctively brace themselves for the blow or even quickly exit the room. Breakout sessions focused on diversity initiatives and social justice and included titles like "How to own your story as a black woman." As a white female, I certainly didn't feel welcome in what was supposed to be an inclusive conference aimed at female empowerment.

The keynote speaker of the conference was Melissa Harris-Perry, former MSNBC opinion show host and well-known social justice advocate. Ms. Perry framed her entire speech around the concept that, in her words, "Every single woman of color would have voted for Hillary Clinton had they not felt too oppressed to go cast a ballot." I knew, after having conducted independent research of my own, her claim was false. The Pew Research Center had proven the opposite, after finding more minority votes were cast for President Trump in 2016 than for Mitt Romney in 2012, while Hillary Clinton's minority support *declined* from President Barack Obama's.[21] *Business Insider* further found 42 percent of all females who voted in 2016 chose President Trump![22] After spending a significant portion of her speech slandering the president, Ms. Perry's rhetoric regarding female conservatives became so despicable that I left the room.

I wanted nothing more than to leave the conference early, but I stuck it out, and I'm glad I did. I began to search for a single truthful or honest fact that added to the credibility of the conference—after all, while the whole week was

---

21 Alec Tyson and Shiva Maniam, "Behind Trump's victory: Divisions by race, gender, education," Pew Research Center, last modified November 9, 2016, https://www.pewresearch.org/fact-tank/2016/11/09/behind-trumps-victory-divisions-by-race-gender-education/.

22 Skye Gould and Rebecca Harrington, "7 charts show who propelled Trump to victory," *Business Insider*, last modified November 10, 2016, https://www.businessinsider.com/exit-polls-who-voted-for-trump-clinton-2016-11.

supposed to be about empowerment, we discussed nothing but oppression. I soon understood the AAUW does not value truth, let alone preach it to their conference attendees. They were more focused on promoting "diversity" than honesty. They didn't want to host an honest discussion about how we can empower one another—that would require actual debate among young women of differing political ideologies, upbringings, and social values. Instead, like college campuses, they wanted a room full of young women who held varying racial, ethnic, and sexual identities—but failed to welcome any diversity of thought. In fact, during the time I spent at the AAUW conference, I met one fellow conservative student. *One.* Considering the overwhelming number of attendees from across the nation, the fact that there were perhaps as few as two of us conservative gals continues to blow me away.

Just like my experience in student government, I felt like a fish out of water. Other than my new friend, it seemed I was the only young woman in attendance with any resemblance of faith in God, our nation, or our president. I would have gained significantly more respect from the hosts and fellow attendees of the conference had I falsely professed the extensive and crippling oppression I was supposed to feel on a daily basis from my "hateful" and white-male-dominated college campus. The isolating nature of the conference and extreme leftist views held by many of my peers was incredibly disheartening. I nearly lost all hope—that is, until I was reminded I would be attending another very different women's conference two weeks later.

Turning Point USA's YWLS was nothing short of a godsend. Unlike AAUW's conference, which pointed out our ideological differences and pitted attendees against one other from the get-go, YWLS began with a single statement by Turning Point USA's founder and president, Charlie Kirk:

> "There will be no safe spaces or trigger warnings here. We encourage you to challenge what you believe and why you believe it."

I was shocked to discover this conference exceeded AAUW in total number of attendees—over 1,000 fellow young women sat beside me in Dallas. Unlike AAUW's obvious love for *physical* aspects of diversity, Turning Point USA seemed to value the true meaning of diversity, welcoming students from all ideologies. There was a wide range of ethnic, racial, religious, and other more obvious distinctions among us as well, but the real value in having such a diverse background of young women displayed itself throughout the weekend, as we shared our beliefs and values held on the inside—not on the outside.

The next several days were overwhelming in the best way. I was a neophyte to this world of activism, having previously only heard of less than half of the speakers and never having attended a political conference before. Notebook and pen in hand, I enthusiastically wrote down nearly every word from each speaker. I was eager to learn as much as I could about articulating my conservative ideology when I returned to campus in the fall. Unlike the depressing message from AAUW, Turning Point USA seemed intent on sharing how I was *already* empowered as a young woman—I didn't need government assistance or radical legislative change to be a leader.

To Turning Point USA, I am a leader, all on my own.

Inspiring female leaders from across the nation shared their stories of building legacies—among them Carly Fiorina (2016 presidential candidate), Lara Trump (daughter-in-law to President Trump), Laura Ingraham (Host of the Ingraham Angle on Fox News), and countless others. Despite having come from wildly unique backgrounds and expertise, these women shared a common message with the attendees: as young women in America, we didn't need government intervention to create our futures. Instead, our futures were ours if we were simply willing to work hard enough for them. We could either perpetuate the false narrative of victimhood preached by the Left, which I had fully experienced two weeks prior, or we could break the cycle through perseverance, hard work, and faith in ourselves.

I fell in love at YWLS.

Turning Point USA was something I had simply stumbled upon thanks to a Facebook advertisement. This organization and conference quickly became so much more to me than an opportunity to meet fellow conservatives. For the first time in my college experience, I knew I had found a community of like-minded individuals who would inspire me to become the best version of myself rather than shame me for the ideas and values I held closest to my heart. I was no longer the "public enemy," as I had come to be known through various leadership positions on my campus. I had the potential to become anything I dreamed, thanks to a newfound faith in myself and my nation. I was prepared to fight for my values, knowing that if I wouldn't, perhaps no one else would. I returned to Colorado, understanding I couldn't possibly be the only conservative student on my campus of 33,000. If I was feeling so isolated and cornered into hiding my beliefs, other students certainly were as well. It was time for a turning point (pun intended) on campus. It was time for students to stand on the front line of our campus culture war.

Turning Point USA fights day in and day out at our nation's universities to preserve conservative values. What began in 2012 as eighteen-year-old Charlie Kirk's dream in a small garage outside of Chicago mushroomed into a worldwide movement embracing the values of freedom and limited government. They are present in thousands of high schools and college campuses nationwide, they've hosted tens of thousands of activism events educating the college community about conservative values, and they've facilitated hundreds of thousands of face-to-face conversations with students about what these values mean.[23] Each year, Turning Point USA campus chapters host prominent conservative speakers on campus to expose students to conservative ideas, which often fail to make it into traditional curriculums.

Unlike well-established conservative or Republican organizations on campus, Turning Point USA is more focused on influencing culture than they are on politics. With eye-catching and controversial slogans like "Big Government Sucks" and "Socialism Sucks," the organization repaints the conservative movement, making it relatable to America's youth—something the right side of the aisle has traditionally failed to do. Instead of offering the typical leadership development opportunities (like knocking on doors or answering phones) that other political organizations offer young people, Turning Point USA uses energizing conferences, engaging

---

23 Turning Point USA, accessed September 30, 2020, https://www.tpusa.com/; "About," Turning Point USA, accessed November 13, 2020, https://www.tpusa.com/about.

community speaker events on campus, and cultivation of community with other young conservatives.

Most recently, they launched an unparalleled production department dominating social media and the internet with daily video content. These videos include everything from *POPlitics* (Alex Clark's daily pop culture Instagram TV show) to hard-hitting interviews with Venezuelan survivors of socialism. Simply put, Turning Point USA is making it *cool* to be a conservative again (and they are the most successful, fastest-growing organization of their kind across the nation).[23] On the Left, no organization compares.

Having just attended YWLS and then binge-watching Turning Point USA's videos throughout the summer, I knew Turning Point USA would be the perfect anecdote to the extreme leftist bias on my campus. I worked with staff members at YWLS to formally established a chapter at CSU after returning to campus that fall. Many of my peers were outraged, particularly those in student government, whom I worked with that year as Speaker. Only the disdain of the faculty and administration rivaled that of my leftist government peers.

I, however, gained newfound confidence in sharing my conservative values on campus. The liberation I experienced when I finally shared them in the ASCSU senate chamber (about the Dakota Access Pipeline resolution) was growing. As I began to regularly interact with others on campus, I felt pride in my beliefs. Freedom, limited government, and free markets were not values I should have ever been ashamed to proclaim; rather, these pillars of Western civilization have improved the world in ways unimaginable throughout most of human history. Turning Point USA reminded me of this truth, and it was now my job to share it with my campus.

At first, our chapter's presence on campus was small, with a handful of dedicated students who had a passion for limited government and individual liberty. In all honesty, even most of the conservative students I knew on campus were still too afraid to ask me about this new organization. One glance at my new "Socialism Sucks" T-shirt in the same font as Bernie Sanders' 2016 campaign logo was enough to scare them away.

When our chapter set up a folding table on our student center plaza, we'd often get quizzical stares and shaking heads (but many smiles, too) in response to our giant "Socialism Sucks" posters and "I ♥ Capitalism" buttons (which you can see in pictures at the end of this book!). I was surprised at the number of curious conservative and liberal students alike who approached me with questions as I collected sign-ups for the chapter.

As the founder of my local Turning Point USA club, I bore the burden of resistance from my community and received more derogatory comments than anyone I knew. I cannot begin to guess how many times I was told to f*ck myself by countless male and female students, and the accusations of racism only grew more frequent. I quickly became more known around campus as "that Turning Point USA girl," and while it was certainly meant as a derogatory label, I wore these words with pride. Liberal friends in the Gender and Ethnic Studies departments soon informed me that "the Turning Point USA girl" was often a subject of conversation in their classrooms, particularly as an example of the ideologies they didn't believe fit into an inclusive environment. Fueled by the knowledge that starting a Turning Point USA chapter on my campus was starting a long-overdue dialogue, I became Chapter President and eventually a part-time employee as a campus coordinator for the organization.

As a junior, for the first time in my college experience, I could tangibly see the tide beginning to change at CSU. Walking around campus, I often overheard students chatting about the new conservative club, wondering if anyone they knew had joined. High-ranking members of the CSU administration began cautiously asking me how my new chapter was doing, curious to see if such an outwardly conservative organization would thrive. Incredibly, professors in my courses would ask their students what they thought about this new club, apparently unaware its founder was sitting right in front of them. Throughout these moments, I simply smiled to myself, overjoyed that I had started the conversation about conservative values on my Colorado campus.

Turning Point USA opened my eyes to a grassroots movement, a new world often hidden in plain sight because of the overbearing leftist presence on college campuses and in the media. After attending my first YWLS conference, I was instantly connected to thousands of other conservative student activists across the nation who were fighting to have a voice at their high school or university. Many of these students had experiences like mine—they had spent many years in their educational communities afraid to publicly advocate for their own values but eventually felt compelled to speak up.

Turning Point USA (and other similar organizations) could

share inspiring stories that take up hundreds of pages, all of which point to one truth—our nation's young adults desperately need exposure to conservative ideas. Some of these organizations dominate social media, others focus on electing conservatives into office, but I have found the most successful conservative organizations take a boots-on-the-ground approach, which is what makes Turning Point USA so effective.

Attending a speech by a conservative speaker on your campus, pinning a "Socialism Sucks" button to your backpack, or showing your friend a conservative video over lunch sparks a healthy conversation about conservative values. It's not about Facebook feed arguments, making phone calls, or knocking on doors. It's about initially sharing conservative values in the smallest ways to pique the interest of one's peers.

And boots-on-the-ground was the specialty of our chapter. Weekly, we hosted public tabling events focused on specific conservative values, such as a conversation at our student center supporting the Second Amendment. We frequently constructed a free-speech wall made from cardboard boxes to encourage students to write whatever they pleased to celebrate their First Amendment rights. Neither our leftist students nor the administration welcomed these events with open arms. However, they were always guaranteed to generate campus-wide conversations about conservative principles one way or another.

Countless times, I've taken part in conversations that have led students to change their minds on issues ranging from border security to taxation principles. Often, I witnessed wide smiles spreading across the faces of my peers as they passed our table overflowing with stickers, buttons, and posters sporting conservative phrases. On many occasions, students and faculty members alike approached our chapter with words of praise and gratitude, thankful that someone—*anyone*—was willing to stand up for conservative values in the first place.

While I had previously thought students on college campuses were approximately 90 percent leftist and extreme in their views, I learned that while this may be true for faculty members, the majority of students on college campuses fall somewhere in the middle on the political spectrum, if they identify with politics at all. It's not hard to convince a fellow student of the validity and logic of the conservative argument if given the proper platform to do so. Charlie Kirk, who's become a friend and mentor, once shared with me that through speaking on campuses across the nation, he's come to discover it's not that college students are blatantly opposed to conservative ideas, they simply are never *exposed* to them—inside their classroom or elsewhere on campus.

Organizations like Turning Point USA, PragerU, Young Americans Against Socialism, and others are facilitating the modern revolution among the next generation to preserve American freedom. I can't believe our nation requires a revolutionary effort to simply maintain the values it so valiantly established a few centuries ago. Yet, here we are. Turning Point has given me, and tens of thousands of students across the nation, limitless opportunities for growth. For me, being a student activist led to public speaking experiences and networking opportunities with the most outspoken and vocal conservative leaders of our time (and even an internship at the White House for the Trump Administration).

Thanks to simple exposure to conservative ideas, at CSU today, more than two hundred students are involved in their Turning Point USA chapter. All it took to catalyze change and create a conservative community was one student willing to stand up and say, "I'm a conservative. I disagree with the campus narrative, and here's why."

It hasn't been easy. In fact, it never is. However, meeting students on my alma mater's campus who were too afraid to come out as conservatives or simply engage in the conversation before the presence of a conservative organization in Fort Collins now feel liberated to embrace their values. That's the most rewarding feeling any college student could ask for.

CHAPTER SEVEN

· · · · · · · · · · · · · · · · · · ·

SPEAKING UP AND SPEAKING OUT

"Isabel is a Nazi. How many million more Jews have to die before we realize that all Nazis deserve to be f*cking shot?"
—CSU STUDENT, 2018

In early 2018, Turning Point USA staff inquired about our CSU chapter's interest in hosting Charlie Kirk as a guest speaker. Enthusiastically, our chapter agreed, knowing the most successful events held by other chapters were speaking events featuring prominent conservatives (like Charlie). As a junior in college, not once had I experienced a well-known conservative speaker coming to campus. However, I had witnessed socialist politician Bernie Sanders (twice!), former MSNBC opinion show host Melissa Harris-Perry, and communist activist Angela Davis speak on campus, thanks to the generosity of my student fee dollars. The leftist bias of my campus faculty and administrators was clear—they weren't interested in diverse political dialogue.

They were interested in facilitating mass leftism.

I was interested in having Charlie Kirk come to speak. However, *nothing* could have prepared me for the chaos, division, and all-out mayhem we would invite for encouraging political dialogue at a public university.

Planning for Charlie's speaking event, particularly during the inaugural months of our chapter, was difficult. I had meetings with the CSU police department and the university events team to discuss security issues, necessary precautions to take, event setup, and the stifling dollar sign associated with it all. Since a prominent conservative speaker hadn't spoken on campus at least since my arrival three years earlier (and likely much longer), it was difficult to predict the level of leftist protests that could take place. However, this was quickly revealed as Antifa began publicly advertising their plans to oppose Charlie's speech. Antifa is an anarchist group (not just an "idea," claimed by former Vice President Joe Biden during the 2020 Presidential Debates[24]) promoting and executing violence against conservative groups and individuals. They call themselves "anti-fascist" but ironically employ many traditionally fascist tactics themselves to silence conservative ideas, like burning books, staging violent protests, destroying property, and brutally attacking those who identify with the right side of the aisle—even to the point of murder as we saw in 2020 in Portland.[25]

---

24 Brittany Bernstein, "Biden Says Antifa Is 'An Idea, Not An Organization' during Presidential Debate," *National Review*, last modified September 29, 2020, https://www.nationalreview.com/news/biden-says-antifa-is-an-idea-not-an-organization-during-presidential-debate/.

25 Sara Ganim and Chris Welch, "Unmasking the leftist Antifa movement," *CNN*, last modified May 3, 2019, https://www.cnn.com/2017/08/18/us/unmasking-antifa-anti-fascists-hard-left/index.html; J.D. Tuccille, "Choose Sides? You Bet. But Antifa and Fascism Are the Same Side.," *Reason*, last modified August 22, 2017, https://reason.com/2017/08/22/choose-sides-you-bet-but-antifa-and-fasc/; Andy Ngo, "A Leftist Mob Attacked Me in Portland," *The Wall Street Journal*, last modified July 2, 2019, https://www.wsj.com/articles/a-leftist-mob-attacked-me-in-portland-11562109768; Masood Farivar, "Antifa Protester Implicated in Killing of Trump Supporter in Oregon," *VOA News*, last modified September 1, 2020, https://www.voanews.com/usa/race-america/antifa-protester-implicated-killing-trump-supporter-oregon.

Shortly after advertising for *Charlie Kirk: Smashing Social-ism at Colorado State University* began, Facebook posts quickly popped up across the state of Colorado, urging the left-wing community to protest the event in its entirety. Antifa's protest, entitled, "Fort Collins Turns Away 'Turning Point USA,'" encouraged students and community members to make a statement against racism. It didn't matter that virtually none of these individuals organizing protests had previously even *heard* of Charlie or were aware of his prior speeches on college campuses—all that mattered was he is a conservative, and therefore, a racist. Their social media graphics blatantly accused students in our chapter of being racists, bigots, nationalists (there's those "-isms" and "-obias" again). The various Antifa groups around the state also claimed Nazis were coming to recruit white supremacists outside of Charlie's speech, which in their opinion was a direct consequence of having a Turning Point USA chapter on campus in the first place.

Due to the radical nature of their accusations, the CSU police department and the Fort Collins police alike expressed their concerns with Antifa's protests. They began including me in additional meetings, specifically regarding the rad-ical nature of Antifa, and I was asked countless questions I felt unprepared to answer. Would I prefer metal detec-tors for attendees of my event inside or outside the student center? Could Charlie come inside the building through a secret passageway in the loading dock? How many days in advance should the concrete barriers outside the building be installed? Who should I call if an all-out brawl were to ensue inside the event? Was I prepared to stop the event at a moment's notice should someone bring a weapon into the building?

As a twenty-year-old student, I was floored. Never would I have imagined I would be responsible for ensuring the safety of hundreds of my peers at a university lecture. Since when did politics become so violent anyway?

My anxiety surrounding the event swelled as flyers popped up around campus.

FORT COLLINS TURNS AWAY "TURNING POINT USA"
FEBRUARY 2 · 5:30PM · LORY STUDENT CENTER
GO TO FACEBOOK.COM/NOCOANCO OR CONTACT US AT NOCOANCO@RISEUR.NET FOR MORE INFORMATION

NO BIGOTRY
NO ETHNOCENTRISM
NO JINGOISM
NO NATIONALISM
NO RACISM
NO XENOPHOBIA
NO TURNING POINT USA
NO CHARLIE KIRK

Honestly, at first, none of Antifa's flyers or Facebook posts bothered me—I was used to the labels, the "-isms" and "-obias," and the slanderous accusations, thanks to my time in student government. Based on the controversies I'd heard of with conservative speaking events on other campuses, I was also expecting some conflict.

Sadly, I found out that Antifa was right about one thing—there would be a controversial, alt-right, and white-supremacist organization known as the Traditionalist Workers Party (TWP) attempting to crash our event. Neither TWP nor Antifa were affiliated with the university or our Turning Point USA chapter in any way. After Antifa began advertising their protest against Charlie, TWP began posting problematic, contentious, racially-charged flyers around campus to counterprotest. Because TWP was counterprotesting Antifa, who was protesting us, they were falsely associated with our chapter by the media and by leftist students, professors, and organizations on campus. As a result, in the weeks leading up to Charlie's on-campus speech, our chapter members and I were put on the defensive, vehemently denying that our organization had any association with TWP. Instead of addressing what we did stand for, we found ourselves explaining what we *didn't* stand for.

I provided many interviews and op-eds on behalf of Turning Point USA that clearly stated the three pillars of our organization: limited government, free markets, and fiscal responsibility—no more, no less. But none of my words seemed to matter. The CSU community was already convinced beyond any doubt that Turning Point USA was using our commitment to these three pillars as a mask to hide our alleged intention of promoting white supremacy and racism. These radical thoughts regarding our chapter's supposed evil intentions began carrying over to our members with their other involvements on campus as our peers and professors began making comments and accusations, which I knew was unacceptable. Like a mother hen, I wanted to protect them from the insanity inevitably coming their way.

To protect our chapter members from these accusations, I engaged in all the media interviews related to the event, and I painfully carried the backlash of Charlie's visit. I began receiving credible threats of violence, even death threats, accompanied by harsh accusations beyond racism. Peers with whom I had worked for nearly three years in student leadership began frequently referring to me as a Nazi and white supremacist. One of the students on my Senate leadership staff (who worked for me!) sent a death threat directed toward me to a mutual friend stating:

> ## Isabel is a Nazi... How many million more Jews have to die before we realize that all Nazi's deserve to be fucking shot?!"

Unfortunately, because his text was not sent directly to me, I was unable to file a report with the campus police, and my friend felt uncomfortable doing so. Overnight, the student government office, where I served as third-in-command Speaker of the Senate, became a dangerous place for me. I was afraid to sit at my desk alone, have any one-on-one meetings with senators, or leave after dark when few people would be present. While the text message was the only clear threat of violence I had received within ASCSU, it became impossible for me to enter the office without everyone suddenly falling silent and whispering about the alleged Nazi and white supremacist leading the senate.

A place that was supposed to serve as an environment of leadership development and personal growth had quickly evolved into a suffocating place of threatened violence.

But the threats didn't stop at the four walls of government. They didn't even stop at the edge of campus.

A few days after the first text message, a random middle-aged woman from a neighboring community—let's call her Sue—whom I suppose to be a leftist activist located my Facebook profile and sent me the following message:

1/31/18, 12:59 PM

if any violence erupts on Friday IT IS YOUR FAULT. Hope no one dies....hope you just get grabbed by the pussy.

 you sick little snowflake

Having two lawyers as parents helps to identify when someone has crossed the line in terms of free speech versus a direct threat. Reference to your status as a protected class—in this case, my status as a female—lands directly in "threat territory." After receiving the Nazi message a few days prior, I was starting to feel pretty rattled, so I called the local police department to report the threat. The Fort

Collins police department quickly responded, and while I chose not to press charges, the police made it clear to Sue that her behavior was unacceptable. Her response to the police was defensive, to say the least. Sue claimed she hadn't threatened me—she had simply quoted our "vile" President of the United States. (Okay, whatever you say, Sue.)

Deciding to move beyond my fear, I prepared for the upcoming event but quickly received the following message from Sue's friend and fellow left-wing community activist:

 Snowy - It's NOT illegal to quote the president. In fact, many lawmakers call that locker room talk.

It appeared Sue had shared her police encounter with her friends, who also found it appropriate to reach out to a college student they had never met to express their hatred for conservatives and their values. So much for the left side of the aisle embracing love and acceptance. These middle-aged, unhappy women whom I had never met were so concerned I would make an impact at CSU, they chose to threaten and bully a twenty-year-old.

I wish I could say this was unbelievable, but this was quickly becoming my new norm. I frequently started screening messages on Facebook and Instagram, and I never went anywhere on campus without my phone, concerned the next threat I would receive would be more physical.

A few days before the event, I did an interview with *The Coloradoan*, an affiliate of *USA Today*. Like many interviews

I did during this time, I strongly disaffiliated the upcoming event featuring Charlie Kirk with the anticipated protests from Antifa and TWP. As the Turning Point USA chapter president, I had already given countless interviews regarding the event and reiterated the fundamental values of our organization. This interview was like any other—pushy journalists and leading questions included—but what made this one unique (and memorable) was what happened afterward.

Apparently, someone was gravely offended by my statements in *The Coloradoan*, or perhaps they were upset about the event taking place to begin with. Regardless, their anger led them to somehow locate my personal contact information and post my personal email address and local apartment address in the comments section of the article on Facebook. To this day, I can't understand how this individual—whom, like Sue and her friend, I had never met before—accessed my local apartment address in Fort Collins; my voter registration and student documents showed my family's home address, which was over an hour away from campus. At the time, I was unfamiliar with "doxing," defined as searching for and publishing private or identifying information about a particular individual (in this case, me) on the internet, typically with malicious intent. But thanks to this individual, I quickly received a crash course on the subject.

No place in my college town felt safe. I was being targeted on campus, in the student government office, by strangers around town, and now even at my own home—the one place that was supposed to be my haven.

Amid all the growing controversy, my parents expressed their concern regarding my safety in my typically friendly college town. I lived alone just off campus in a one-bedroom apartment and walked or rode my bike from my office in student government or from a late-night study session every day. Further, I was only twenty years old and thus couldn't obtain a concealed carry license or purchase a firearm for my apartment to protect myself. So, my mom decided to stay with me in my apartment and attend classes for a few days leading up to Charlie's event. As sweet and caring as this gesture was, no twenty-year-old college student wants to be in a situation where their mom *needs* to go to school with them to keep them safe. (Cue extreme embarrassment.)

I'm not trying to gain sympathy points or to woefully complain about my prior situation. Despite being threatened, I never felt victimized. I share these stories because they reveal the daily reality of thousands of conservative student activists like me. Outright violence is condoned, even applauded, not only toward the prominent conservative speakers bold enough to lecture on campuses but sometimes even more so to the local students associated with bringing them there. Speakers and political influencers often share the stories of the insane and enraged protests occurring outside of their speeches, but the stories of violence and targeting propagated toward the students hosting the event before and after these speakers leave are rarely, if ever, shared through the media. When a conservative speaker comes to a public college campus, the conservative students pay for it. These brave students are on the front line, preserving conservative values on our nation's campuses, often jeopardizing their own reputations, social status, and even physical safety in the process.

On February 2, 2018, the day had finally arrived for Charlie to speak at CSU. Throughout the day, it seemed every class on campus was, in some way, shape, or form, discussing the event and unprecedented controversy associated with the guest speaker. An email from our administration was distributed to the entire campus, urging minority students to avoid the heart of campus (to keep students safe from "white supremacists") and encouraging all students to take advantage of free counseling and therapy. As you may expect, not once did this email suggest that students expand their exposure by attending the event. Again, I saw the truth of the supposed "liberal arts education." Universities aren't really interested in exposing students to diverse thoughts or new perspectives. They're simply interested in exposing their students to a single way of thinking—the way of the Left.

A few hours before the event, I was inside our student center auditorium, setting up signs and double-checking audiovisual equipment. I heard sirens and loud protests outside. Apparently, during the few hours leading up to Charlie's speech, chaos had erupted. Just outside the auditorium, hundreds of Antifa activists and TWP members, alongside students and faculty members, loudly and violently expressed their outrage. They were holding posters and even punching their adversaries. Ironically, inside the venue, there was no violence in any shape or form! Over seven hundred students, faculty members, and individuals from our community had peacefully gathered to hear Charlie speak (it happened to be the largest campus gathering ever for him, up to that point).

Charlie delivered a thought-provoking, intellectual, and lighthearted presentation that wowed the audience. Conservative thinkers and liberals alike showed up to be respectfully challenged. Following his prepared speech, attendees had the opportunity to ask Charlie whatever question they desired; no one was forbidden from expressing their views, *especially* if they disagreed with Charlie. In fact, if a student outwardly expressed disagreement with Charlie's values, he invited them to skip the line and come to the front to ask their question. The audience was shocked—true and respectful debate was happening for the first time in many years at CSU.

The juxtaposition between the *real* event—the peaceful and important exchange of ideas—with the protests outside that had *nothing* to do with the actual event was shocking. By observing the difference between the protests raging outside versus engaging in the inspiring exchange of diverse ideas inside, I witnessed the irony of conservative lectures on today's college campuses. The "danger" that leftist students, faculty, and community members accuse prominent conservatives of bringing to campuses would never happen in the first place if far-left individuals did not riot in response to their presence (the National Guard had to be there to keep the peace!).

The only true "danger" that occurred from Charlie's actual speech—violent protests propagated by Antifa activists excluded—was the "harmful" exposure to new ideas offered to students. (The horror!) Universities should be encouraging events featuring conservative intellectuals, so students on both sides of the aisle can expand their foundational values and perspectives on the world. Shouldn't universities be promoting this type of discourse? Even if universities were honest about their intentions to teach leftist ideas to students, wouldn't they want to bring as many conservative speakers to campus as possible, simply to disprove conservative ideas?

Unfortunately, the media (from our campus newspaper to Denver's 9News station) focused on the rioting and political polarization that had nothing to do with Charlie's speech. I, however, felt pride in what our small group of student leaders was able to accomplish through a single event.

Following the event, hundreds of students approached our chapter leadership, thanking us for giving them an outlet and community of like-minded students. Some students spoke through tears, while others had enormous smiles on their faces, sharing that they finally felt like they belonged on their college campus for the first time. Professors scurried to the front of the room, thanking me for creating a space for conservative thought they couldn't always create in their classrooms. The overwhelmingly positive feedback immediately erased any uneasiness from the threats and negative responses.

A wide smile spread across *my* face. *This* was why I had started a Turning Point USA chapter in Fort Collins—to give conservative students a home, a place to call their own, and to provide a platform where students could challenge individual perspectives. The tide was changing, and we were just getting started.

CHAPTER EIGHT

. . . .

CHANGE MY MIND

"Black people are not a monolith. You need to understand this. We are not ideological slaves. I do not have to think like her, and she does not have to think like me because of the color of our skin."
—Candace Owens at Colorado State University, 2018

The extreme antagonism against conservatives continued, on campus and in the broader Fort Collins community, even after Charlie's speech. The overwhelming success and high attendance only encouraged the Left to push back harder against the conservatives—even their fellow students.

In response to growing allegations of our status as a "white supremacist organization" on campus, we forged ahead. Just a few months following Charlie's speech, our chapter hosted Candace Owens for a "Change My Mind" style tabling event. It was one of her first campus events. At the time, Candace was the Director of Communications for Turning Point USA, and she remains a prominent black female conservative leader.

The "Change My Mind" concept was started by Steven Crowder, a hilarious conservative personality and host of *Louder with Crowder*, a popular talk show on TheBlaze Radio Network. Steven's concept began with his visits to college campuses where, instead of lecturing to students and faculty members, he would set up a table and film interviews with students, daring them to debate him (and "change his mind") on a certain topic. Previous episodes of "Change My Mind" have included "Hate Speech Isn't Real: Change My Mind," "Trump is Not a Fascist: Change My Mind," and even "I'm Pro-Life: Change My Mind." In general, hundreds of students interact with him on any given day on college campuses throughout the nation, and he *has* changed his mind on a handful of issues thanks to well-educated students, but it would seem, more often than not, he changes theirs.

After observing the success of these events, our chapter leadership decided to give it a shot.

Candace's event was titled *Turning Point USA is Not a White Supremacist Organization: Change My Mind*. Instead of marketing Candace's visit to campus in advance, we kept her guest appearance a secret until the day of her event in April 2018, when we unveiled our plans by setting up a table on our student center plaza and through video promotions on social media.

Like Charlie's event on campus, Candace's "Change My Mind" debate with students was successful beyond our chapter's deepest hopes. Roughly five hundred students and faculty members came to hear and challenge what Candace had to say, and the response was shocking. Candace asked them why an alleged "white supremacist organization" would hire a black female communications director, or why the color of one's skin predisposes one to success or failure in the United States. Some of the students responded with rehearsed talking points from their classes on campus, but many simply took in the information with an open mind. Many minority students who identified with the Left examined the false nature of many rumors about Turning Point USA's alleged "racist" nature and denied them. Other students simply pushed back against Candace and Turning Point with even more resistance. Members of leftist student organizations called the campus police to disband our event, but because of the trusty First Amendment (thanks, Founding Fathers) and our status as a public university, the police could do nothing but stay and watch. Candace's bravery of diving headfirst into the lion's den was inspiring to conservative and liberal students alike, and her boldness spiked resistance among my peers.

One group of students who were largely involved with the Young Democratic Socialists of America (YDSA) became notably belligerent over Candace's presence on campus. Erica, a Hispanic graduate student studying ethnic studies, interrupted Candace's conversation with someone else, screaming that Candace was allowing her black body to be used by Turning Point USA to pretend to care about minorities. "How do you think your [black] sisters feel about this? Angela Davis? Do you know Audre Lorde?" she asked Candace, in a combative tone.

Candace's response was brilliant. "Black people are not a monolith. I can think differently from Angela Davis. She can think differently from the black girl who's standing right there. *She* can think differently from the black guy who I just had a conversation with. You need to understand this. We are not ideological slaves. I do not have to think like her, and she does not have to think like me because of the color of our skin. The fact that you think that way is not very healthy."

In response, Erica screamed incoherently in Candace's face, likely because her ethnic studies program had taught her that minorities could not possibly think conservatively. Truthfully, based on her educational background, I don't even blame Erica for her response. It's all she'd ever been taught!

Following the event, Erica gave a quote to the *Rocky Mountain Collegian*, our student newspaper on campus, stating, "There's this assumption that even if you're a person of color, if you identify as a marginalized identity, you somehow can't perpetuate oppression, and can't perpetuate white supremacy, and that is absolutely inaccurate."

After reading the article and obtaining video footage of the encounter, Candace posted a video on Facebook of her exchange with Erica.

The Left came unglued.

Erica attended the following week's student senate meeting in tears and screamed at our student government leaders regarding the post. She claimed that she had been doxed by Candace Owens and demanded that the student government disband Turning Point USA and bar the club from campus. Having been doxed myself a few months prior, I wasn't stunned by her outburst. Erica clearly didn't understand what doxing was—after providing your name in a public interview, it's fair game for someone to share. Had Candace posted Erica's phone number or address, I would have understood the doxing allegation, but otherwise, no one would buy her story for one second. (Plus, if she hadn't wanted her name to be associated with her words, she should have avoided the camera-saturated event, and she shouldn't have given her name and statement to the campus newspaper!)

After all this time, the concept that conservative ideas were "dangerous" and "harmful" to students had not ceased by any means. Still, the Left's resistance to conservative groups and speakers on the CSU campus did not dissuade Turning Point USA or me. In response to the successful events with both Charlie Kirk and Candace Owens, more students joined our chapter. Energized, we planned another campus speech— this time, featuring PragerU founder, Dennis Prager. I was just getting started.

Like Charlie and Candace's events, the Left had a meltdown at even the concept of hosting someone on campus as prominently conservative as Dennis. Students met with members of the administration and student government for weeks attempting to prevent the event. Professors from across the university urged their students not to attend, claiming to their students, "Those white supremacist students are at it again." In the weeks leading up to his campus visit, op-eds were published in the student newspaper, falsely accusing Dennis of advocating for marital rape, being Islamophobic, and most absurdly, comparing him to a Nazi. Posters began popping up around campus advertising these false allegations without a shred of evidence, demanding "action" after stating:

"DENNIS PRAGER HAS PROMOTED THE MORALITY OF AMERICAN SLAVERY, ADVOCATED FOR MARITAL RAPE, DENIED POLICE KILLINGS OF BLACK PEOPLE, ARGUED THAT MUSLIMS CANNOT BE TRUSTED, PORTRAYED HOMOSEXUALITY AS A DEATH CULT, ENCOURAGED BEATING CHILDREN, AMONG OTHER HORRIBLE PRACTICES."

I should mention that Dennis is a well-respected theologian and a prominent intellectual within the Jewish community. (Could these accusations be any more baseless?)

Despite their best attempts, the efforts to silence Dennis's speech were futile. In October 2018, over 1,200 students, faculty members, and individuals came to Dennis's event, and our chapter's campus event became one of the largest in Turning Point USA history.

As I looked around the room during his speech, my heart swelled with pride seeing students of all backgrounds and ideologies—including many wearing "Black Lives Matter" and "Bernie 2016" T-shirts—sitting peacefully during the speech, then racing to the front of the line for questions. The dialogue Turning Point USA brought to campus seemed to benefit all members of the community, expand our education, and reveal the commonality among students, not the differences.

Today, from my position as a spokesperson for Turning Point USA, who speaks with college students across the nation and listens to their testimonies, I know that attending events with prominent conservatives like Charlie Kirk, Candace Owens, and Dennis Prager is the highlight of many students' academic year, and often their entire college experience. When I was a student hosting events at Colorado State University, many of my peers drove hours from other universities and even states to attend them, eager for a diverse viewpoint. For a few hours, these students had the opportunity to experience a fearless leader sharing values and perspectives with the world—and they're reminded it's okay to promote conservatism and share their values themselves. They aren't evil, they aren't racist, they aren't [insert "-ism or "-obia" here]—they're just themselves, adorned with MAGA hats and "Socialism Sucks" T-shirts, and surrounded by the few students on campus who outwardly agree with them.

Attending these events, however, can be risky—and not just for students. To show your face attending and supporting a speech given by a conservative activist means risking your status on campus, especially for faculty members and professors. While standing in the back of the event space during Dennis's speech, a campus police officer I have worked with to prepare for Turning Point USA events quietly approached me and shared that his wife was a huge fan of Dennis Prager. Excitedly, I asked where she was. I would, of course, take her backstage to meet him! He half-smiled and softly replied that she was a member of the CSU faculty, and she felt uncomfortable. She believed others would single her out for showing support for Dennis. Even the idea of campus faculty members fearing for their livelihood should they express their political affiliation should lead our nation's administrators to pause and consider campus culture.

Similarly, a handful of business professors approached me later in the evening, profusely thanking us for hosting

Dennis on our campus. As conservative professors, they're timid about sharing their beliefs with their students and particularly with their colleagues and supervisors. After thanking me for hosting the event, they whispered with a wink that they always teach the importance of capitalism in their classes (socialism wasn't going to win over their students on their watch!).

Hosting Dennis Prager on campus after having two prior rewarding and fruitful events was the perfect way to round out my experience as the Turning Point USA chapter president at CSU. Dennis's kind and honest persona was contagious, and he certainly challenged each attendee to embrace logic and reason over maniacal anger directed toward conservatives. One by one, Dennis debunked each accusation thrown at him from statements cited in our student newspaper, spoken in student government, and hastily strewn on posters. He did not "hate the gay community," but instead is a godfather to a child of a gay couple. He did not advocate for marital rape and cited hundreds of previous podcasts, radio shows, and speeches in which he vehemently denied these claims. He did not promote the morality of American slavery—in fact, he hated slavery as much as any other sane human being. Most notably, he did not advocate for Nazis—as a respected member of the Jewish community, he has perhaps condemned the Nazi party more frequently than he has taken a breath.

Other than hosting such a respected intellectual, the most inspiring aspect of our chapter's event featuring Dennis was the makeup of the attendees themselves. Students and faculty members alike, from Black Lives Matter activists to prominent student leaders in the SDPS offices—who

I had witnessed aggressively protesting Charlie's speech just nine months before—instead chose to attend the event, apparently to hear what Dennis had to say. I had promised attendees that if they disagreed with Dennis's speech at any point during the evening, they could move to the front of the line during the question-and-answer portion of the event. To my surprise, dozens of students took advantage of the opportunity. Just like our previous events, productive dialogue and debate inspired every member of the audience. Unlike Charlie and Candace's presentations, there were virtually no raging protests nearby. I was shocked. Somehow, our Turning Point USA chapter—without the help of our university faculty and administration—had managed to convince even the most far-left students that exposure to diverse ideas was a beneficial and positive aspect of the college experience. I was proud of the progress our campus had made in less than a year.

I know the Turning Point USA chapter at CSU will only continue to thrive in the coming years. Conversation about conservative values at my alma mater will persevere, thanks to passionate students continuing to lead the conservative movement on campus and faculty members committed to upholding the First Amendment.

Students who are willing to host intellectuals on campus to expose their peers and professors to conservative values— often for the first time—are the conservative movement's quiet, unsung heroes. These students risk their friendships, their reputations among professors and faculty, and their opportunities for leadership in student roles. Sometimes, they even willingly jeopardize their personal safety for the sake of educating their peers with truth—truth that often their professors' extreme views overshadow or dismiss altogether. These students are inspiring, and I am deeply proud to have been labeled "that Turning Point USA girl" from founding my local chapter and consequently following through on my promises to host Charlie, Candace, and Dennis on campus. Looking back, the threats, the danger I felt, and even the fear I lived with after being doxed stand as proof that I made a difference. Plus, because I was willing to bear the worst of the backlash, I created a space for others like me to gather in community and in pride of their values. More importantly, we created a venue to change the minds of our peers.

Given the opportunity, I would do it all over again, exactly the same way. My experiences thickened my skin for my future endeavors as a changemaker on college campuses and beyond. Of course, the Left is sure to have a meltdown in response to conservative students and the events they host, which is exactly what happened at CSU, but we conservative young adults aren't done changing minds quite yet.

CHAPTER NINE

. . . .

COMING UNGLUED

"We will fight for the dismantling of Turning Point USA at CSU. We demand that they be banned from our campus and our education. To the administration, we ask you if you will support us in this campaign, or will you continue to allow white supremacy to thrive on our campus? The choice is yours."

—CSU STUDENTS AGAINST WHITE SUPREMACY, 2018

"Trump Derangement Syndrome," or TDS, refers to the hysteric mania leftist activists—particularly young leftists—experience when they are unable to wrap their heads around President Donald Trump's success in being elected to the presidency and what he accomplished in office. The TDS term became a household phrase throughout the early years of President Donald Trump's 2016 presidency. This derangement has, in my experience, ballooned to include all aspects of the conservative movement, particularly on America's college campuses. A scientist by education, I have decided to coin this new phenomenon, "Conservative Derangement Syndrome," or CDS.

CDS has telltale symptoms, including irrational screaming, bouts of depressive activity, and demands of removal from any triggering conservative presence near or around the patient. A CDS-positive leftist is likely to vote for Bernie Sanders, tweet about the importance of socialism fifty-plus times per day, and frequently direct threats or cuss words toward conservatives in public. At CSU, the leftist student activists on campus diagnosed with the disease all experienced one common prevailing symptom—they were coming unglued.

The presence and success of conservative student activists at CSU, particularly through Turning Point USA, had caused quite a stir on our Fort Collins campus. No longer did the Left dominate every conversation. For the first time, conservative students felt emboldened to speak up in their classrooms, around campus, and even on social media.

At first, I had hoped having successful student groups on both sides of the aisle would strengthen opportunities for politically diverse debate and conversation. After seeing the Left's reaction at our first event, I knew this dream would take time to be realized. On today's campuses, conservative students aren't debating *liberals*—kind, open-minded individuals willing to debate, converse, and disagree. Conservative students are up against *leftists*—who believe certain free speech (especially conservative speech) ought to be restricted as "hate speech." Leftists are vehemently unwilling to even stand in the vicinity of conservatives unless attempting to provoke them with violence.

Following Turning Point USA's first successful speaking event at CSU with Charlie Kirk, the community-wide rhetoric continued. Apparently, Charlie was still a "white supremacist," and Turning Point USA activists had promoted a "Nazi group." For weeks, professors cited the existence of our chapter and the presence of alleged "Nazi and white supremacist students" (i.e., chapter members) on our campus as evidence of racism in our community. Often, members of our chapter would be sitting in class as their professors uttered these angry diatribes, and the students would sit shell-shocked, terrified that their Turning Point USA membership would be "outed."

On a number of occasions, I entered a classroom on campus and saw the professor's notes on the board from a previous course, with arrows clearly drawn between the words "Turning Point USA" and "white supremacy," knowing yet another "educational" discussion had ensued about our club minutes earlier. Students happily obliged these accusations, rapidly circulating and inflating them. This was when my story as a conservative student became truly ugly.

Just after Charlie's event in early 2018, and before Candace Owens had hosted her conversation on campus that fall, a group of my friends in student government approached me in my office. They sported handfuls of buttons they had picked up from a table of students none of us knew in the center of campus, with some sporting the phrase "F*ck White Supremacy" and others containing our chapter logo with a slash through it. I burst into laughter, knowing this was perhaps the most absurd thing to have occurred in the wake of Charlie's successful speech.

Curious, I wandered outside to ask these students about their buttons and learn about their demands for action at

CSU. At the time, these students amazingly had no idea who I was. They especially weren't aware that I was the chapter president of Turning Point USA, which gave me an opportunity to get the real story about who they were and what they were fighting. The best part? I caught the entire interaction on video.

I approached their table, clad with a massive homemade banner reading "Students Against White Supremacy" and scattered with anti-Turning Point USA buttons, to find a few (ironically, all white) students in jean jackets bejeweled with their buttons conversing with others about their new coalition. One young woman (whom we'll call Sarah, as I never learned her name) explained that Students Against White Supremacy, or SAWS, was a conglomerate of a few other student organizations at CSU, including the Young Democratic Socialists of America, who had decided to come together to campaign against "the stuff that's been going on around campus."

Their other core mission was to, in Sarah's words, "bring awareness about Turning Point USA on campus, because, um, on other campuses where they've been elected to student government…they have done things like make it so you can't protest, and you get fined if you do…and they expand free speech zones." Hmm. This seemed counterintuitive to me. Wouldn't expansion of free speech zones allow *more* protesting without restriction?

Curious, I asked Sarah if she knew which "other campuses" were dealing with these supposed free speech issues. "Um, I don't know exactly; I can ask one of them," she responded, gesturing to her fellow SAWS activists. *Unsurprising. Let's move on,* I thought. I asked, "So, why the buttons specific to Turning Point USA?" wondering why my peers were so focused on ridding our campus of a single club. The following exchange was, to say the least, enlightening. (Grammar fell by the wayside as our conversation continued.)

Sarah: "Uh, because they have a couple people running for ASCSU right now, um, they are associated with Turning Point USA, and so we don't want them to be elected."

Me: "I really like your message, I mean, totally with you in terms that white supremacy is a horrible thing, and it should not be affecting our campus in any way, shape, or form. I'm curious why one specific club on our campus is being targeted by your campaign versus everybody else on campus."

Sarah: "Alright, well, it also has to do with what they stand for."

Me: "What do they stand for?"

Sarah: "Well, they kind of, uh, position themselves as an organization that, uh, only discusses economic issues, um, when in reality they often discuss other issues."

Me: "Like what?"

Sarah: "Such as, uh, sorry, I'm really tired right now. Such as, um, sweatshops in third-world countries and how..."

Me: "When has that been talked about on our campus by Turning Point USA?"

Sarah: "Oh, when Charlie Kirk was here."

Me: "What are the other things that Turning Point talks about that bother you?"

Sarah: "Ummmmmm, I have a list somewhere on my phone; I can't remember right now. He [Charlie Kirk] also says that white privilege is a myth."

Me: "Well, you know, I was curious because Turning Point USA is an organization that focuses on economic issues, so I was surprised. Have you ever attended a meeting of that organization? Or do you know someone who has?"

Sarah: "No."

Ah yes, the truth came out. *Of course* Sarah had never attended one of our meetings, been at Charlie's speech a few weeks prior, or even done any research on what Turning Point USA stood for! She couldn't even articulate why our chapter bothered her and instead referred me to a "list on her phone" that she "couldn't remember" with regards as to why our organization was considered so evil and racist. This young woman had done no research and had zero previous experience with a massive, nationwide organization making waves for conservatives. Nonetheless, she felt emboldened enough to actively advertise a countermovement against Turning Point USA for being a "white supremacist" organization and was attempting to recruit fellow leftist students to attend their first meeting.

At this point, a small group of students had gathered around the SAWS table, and a young woman from the crowd spoke up, claiming to have attended a Turning Point USA chapter meeting. Serving as the chapter president, it was *my* job to know every member of our organization and host every meeting, and I had never met this young woman in my life. She certainly had never signed up for our chapter, let alone attended a meeting. For the sake of anonymity, we'll call this young woman—the supposed expert on Turning Point USA and Charlie Kirk—Laura.

Laura: "I have [attended a meeting]. They talk a lot about how race, ya know, is kind of becoming anti-white. What turned me off, cuz I, I, I, I went through a nice phase where I was like, 'Oh, a Turning Point sounds like a nice place, like all they're talking about is like, economics and whatnot.' But as soon as I was here for Charlie Kirk and just like, witnessing everything that went down, I wasn't here for when the actual NAZIS came out, but the fact that those people felt like this was, like they felt like it was now okay for them to out themselves as a Nazi because a speaker was here, that put me off."

Me: "Did you go in to the [Charlie Kirk] talk?"

Laura: "No, because I was out here. They [Charlie Kirk, Turning Point USA] can denounce them [Nazis] all they want, but the fact that white supremacists feel comfortable coming out [makes them a racist organization]."

So...

- Laura hadn't attended a chapter meeting.
- She had instead attended the Charlie Kirk *event*.
- (But wait, there's more!)
- She hadn't even attended the event—she'd been outside at the protest, claiming to understand everything that occurred during Charlie's speech that evening!

It immediately became very clear to me none of these students had the slightest understanding of what Turning Point USA even was, not to mention what they stood for or believed in. But these facts had no bearing on their supposed "expertise" on the subject—all they needed to know was that it was a right-leaning organization to know that it must be a white supremacist organization, too.

Pretty soon, a young man, we'll call him Larry, who had been advertising at the table alongside Sarah and was a known leader of the Young Democratic Socialists of America group on campus, began sharing his own two cents on the matter. Larry's central point was that it didn't matter how many times someone like Charlie or an organization like Turning Point USA denounced white supremacist groups—all that mattered was these two demographics shared an interest in the same "policy initiatives" that were directly propagating racism in our country. This casual link alone was sufficient to label all conservatives on campus as white supremacists.

Larry: "They identify with so many of the same policy positions. It's because they see their own politics reflected in that figure. That figure can, like, denounce, but they can't create that actual separation."

Me: "So, what policy positions do white supremacists align with, then?"

Larry: "Border wall is a big one. Um, the denial of white privilege is another big connection between the two groups. Um, same with, like, usually white supremacists align economically with conservatives as well, but only for certain communities. They would like to see white people engaging in capitalism, ya know? Um, but like everyone outside their circle is kicked out. Just because Turning Point denounces them [white supremacists], does not mean that those connections in terms of ideology aren't there."

Me: "So how do you think you get rid of those connections? At what point would it be okay to not have to hand out these buttons anymore?"

Larry: "Um, if speakers such as Charlie Kirk, who act as an encouraging force for white supremacists, distance themselves from those policies. These people [Nazis] identify with that movement and come out [as Nazis] because they feel represented in it and they're more welcomed."

Me: "Even though, every step of the way, the speaker said, 'This is absolutely ridiculous and should not be a part of American culture?' So, he would have to not be a conservative or not hold the policy positions he has to make sure that this wouldn't be a problem?"

Larry: "In terms of a border wall, yes."

It took a while, but the truth came out.

Larry had little knowledge of what traditionally conservative policies were or what they were attempting to solve. But Larry had it all figured out—"conservative," to him, was another code word for an ambiguous group of white supremacists.

Larry, I later discovered, was a student in the political science department, which I suppose must have taught that conservatives propagate racist policies. As most know, the most successful implementation of "white supremacist" policies was initiated by the fascist regime of the Nazi party. While many avenues of formal education teach students that fascism is a concept of the extreme right-wing, fascism is truthfully a manifestation of the extreme left—complete government control, banning hate speech, certain phrases, and more. There is a fantastic PragerU video on the subject that I would suggest to anyone who's been taught that fascism is a "conservative" principle.[26]

Anyone could observe this same pattern of conversation that I had with the SAWS student activists during the question-and-answer portion of conservative speakers' events on campuses, especially during informal, conversational events (like Candace's "Change My Mind" event). Most of the time, leftist students like Sarah, Laura, and Larry sound like they know what they are talking about by using big words and phrases most people only slightly understand, but if an educated and empowered conservative asks enough questions, they have no idea how to respond. This was proven to me through Sarah's forgetful nature when it came to why Turning Point USA upset her so much, through Laura's false expertise on Charlie's speech (which was really centered around her attendance at the protest outside), and Larry's twisted understanding of how policy truly worked by assuming all conservative ideas were somehow rooted in racism or white supremacy. The ugly truth, however, is that, often, it doesn't matter how many times you debunk their central arguments by asking probing questions or how many times you denounce white supremacy. As long as the Left knows

---

26 Dinesh D'Souza, "Is Fascism Left or Right?" PragerU, video published December 4, 2017, https://www.prageru.com/video/is-fascism-right-or-left/.

you are a conservative, you are tied to racism and the Nazi party by leftist students.

Walking away from my comical exchange with the SAWS, I had to chuckle. This new organization shouldn't have called themselves "Students Against White Supremacy" (which, by the way, every sane person would be a part of; as *no one* in their right mind believes in the supremacy of one race over another in the twenty-first century). Instead, they should have named themselves "Students Against Turning Point USA." They weren't even interested in taking down the other conservative or right-leaning organizations on campus, including College Republicans, Young Americans for Liberty, or Students for Life—SAWS was honed in on the complete and total destruction of Turning Point USA on CSU's campus. Clearly, they weren't the most educated group of young adults, despite their many years in formal education, based on their lack of knowledge and twisted thinking when it came to how different political groups aligned with policy positions.

I was convinced their movement wouldn't grow. Certainly, educated young people would have enough common sense to understand the blatant lies of such a group and protect the rights of all students regardless of political affiliation; surely, no *faculty* and administration could buy into the SAWS.

However, it seemed that once more, I had underestimated the level of pure insanity.

Students Against White Supremacy, or SAWS, refused to become a registered student organization with the university because it would have harmed their anarchic approach by forcing them to "play nice."

Soon, SAWS began to target conservative student activists at CSU with tactics never witnessed by any Turning Point USA chapter. With the intention of running conservative ideas off campus entirely, SAWS began to fundamentally change the way the student body viewed conservative students at CSU. After heavily recruiting students from the SDPS offices and various educational departments across campus, including the ethnic studies department and the graduate school, they launched an Antifa-like social media campaign, smearing our organization and labeling our students as white supremacists. The campaign entailed cartoons and graphics made by their student leaders. They posted images like this all around campus, directed at our club:

SAWS quickly began identifying which students were involved with Turning Point USA and subsequently started screenshotting and posting their photos and Facebook profiles all over social media to prevent conservative students on our campus from achieving positions of leadership, particularly in student government. While leftists at other universities across the nation had targeted and protested Turning Point USA student groups and chapter presidents, there had never been an organized attempt by an established group of students to reveal chapter participants and thwart their potential success on campus. We were in uncharted territory.

Sadly, it seemed my prior findings regarding the true intentions of diversity initiatives being geared toward division rather than inclusion were correct after all. This conclusion suddenly manifested itself. Students who had years of experience as leaders in diversity programs through the SDPS offices, PLP, student government, and departmental programs were now part of SAWS, a coalition that was supposedly creating a more inclusive environment on our campus. In reality, SAWS directly advocated for the division of students by pitting politically uneducated students against conservatives by labeling them as white supremacists. Once more, diversity was not being celebrated through alleged diversity advocates. Instead of unifying our campus, they were dividing us.

Nothing illustrated this concept more clearly throughout my college experience than a university-sanctioned event known as *CSUnite: No Place 4 H8*. Earlier in the 2017–2018 academic year, there had been a handful of documented incidences of true racial intolerance. The university labeled these as "bias-related incidents." A noose was hung in the hallway of a residence hall overseen by a black resident assistant, and swastikas were drawn on the dorm room doors of a few Jewish freshman students. (Obviously, no student should have to endure such bigotry on a college campus.)

In response to these bias-related incidents, the university administration scheduled CSUnite to bring students together as one community. The event entailed a march from one end of the campus to another, at which point attendees would gather in front of a stage in the heart of campus to hear from speakers from across the faculty and administration, including many university vice presidents and the president. Overall, CSUnite sought to unify our community as one after hateful events had ensued on campus—a noble endeavor, and I was supportive of the cause.

As a cohesive Turning Point USA chapter, our activists decided to attend in solidarity with our community. Like our administration, we believed everyone had a place to call their own within the CSU community, and we wanted to speak out against actual events of intolerance. Importantly, we believed our presence at the event would help communicate that we are not racists nor white supremacists—we actively stand against such behavior. So, we took our place for the march among thousands of our peers from the university. We felt we could take our place in support of our collective community, regardless of our political differences.

Spoiler alert: we were wrong.

Halfway through the march, we began to hear faint chanting

that became progressively louder. As we approached the sound, we could make out: "No Nazis, No KKK, No TPUSA," being shouted by—you guessed it—our friends from Students Against White Supremacy. They had draped a massive banner with these words over the side of a central building and had begun chanting as soon as they identified members of our chapter in the crowd. It seemed the event had failed to complete its mission as advertised—to create a space where there was no place for hate. There was a tangible feeling of hatred in the air surrounding the participants upon confronting this sign. Our chapter members, including myself, began to feel very uncomfortable about our presence at the event.

And it was about to get worse.

As thousands of students at the event began to gather near the stage and prepared to hear from members of the university administration, SAWS activists dispersed and distributed flyers sharing their core mission with the crowd—to rid our university of "evil conservatives." On one side, these flyers told students Turning Point USA was a "white supremacist" organization. They stated our student body refused to align with white supremacists under a "false flag of unity" suggested by the CSUnite program put together by the university. The full text of the front side of the flyer stated:

The institution is built on White Supremacy

i.   The actions and words of Turning Point USA directly encourage White Supremacy on campus
ii. Bias-related incidents are acts of White Supremacy

iii. The University has made the choice to do nothing, despite their power to make real change

iv. This has created an unsafe space for marginalized students on campus and puts the burden of healing from trauma onto those students.

v. Therefore, there will be no false flags of unity with students who perpetuate White Supremacy

vi. We demand for TPUSA to be dismantled or kicked off campus

As if that wasn't bad enough, the flip side of the flyer contained a lengthy paragraph explaining the inherent racism allegedly found on our campus, which was supposedly perpetuated by organizations like Turning Point USA.

Just after the CSU Vice President for Student Affairs gave a speech, and before the microphone could be passed to the next speaker (the CSU President and Chancellor), this insane group of students (SAWS), not even recognized as a formal student organization, stormed the stage. Clad in masks and dark clothing, they proceeded to state the following, uninterrupted by the administration, which I recorded on video:

"Why disrupt? We, the students of this university, claim this time for our voices to be heard. Today we have been gathered under the false notion of unity at CSU. A ruse that seeks to veil the divisions and hatred that boils with the heat of white supremacy and leaves students of color burned and scarred by their experiences here.

We, Students Against White Supremacy, seek to end hate crimes that occur repeatedly on our campus. Through the exposure of white supremacy, our campaign will utilize the power of student voices and action united in nonhierarchical coalitions to liberate our campus from white supremacy.

In order to do so, we must first acknowledge that white supremacy is built into the very foundation of this institution. It is our responsibility to acknowledge that the land we use as our campus is occupied and taken from Indigenous tribes. In this way, we contend with our settler colonial position and honor the Apache, Arapaho, Cheyenne, Pueblo, Kiowa, Shoshone, and Navajo Nations. Since the time that these lands were stolen and this campus constructed, structures and ideologies that position white people as human and 'others' as nonhuman savages have been allowed to thrive.

The so-called 'bias-related incidents' on campus are, in fact, acts of hatred by white supremacists. Despite having the power to create real and radical change by acknowledging these hate crimes for what they are and addressing them appropriately, our university has made the choice to pull a veil over them and pretend like they don't affect the lives of the students who attend CSU.

Furthermore, organizations like Turning Point USA have been allowed to infiltrate our campus via student organizations and student government. The words and actions of Turning Point USA directly support and encourage white supremacy on this campus, and they continue to go unchecked while students of color are left with the burden of healing from the trauma caused by this hateful rhetoric.

Now exhaustion, passion, and love have driven us to do what our administration has failed to by hearing and meeting our demands for an inclusive, equitable, and safe education for everyone. We will not unite under a false flag of unity with students who perpetuate white supremacy. Instead, we will hold them accountable for their actions, and we will fight for the dismantling of Turning Point USA at CSU. We demand that they be banned from our campus and our education. To the administration, we ask you if you will support us in this campaign, or will you continue to allow white supremacy to thrive on our campus? The choice is yours."

Our university's top administrative officials on stage stood silently, stunned by the brazen decision by an unrecognized student group to seize the stage currently occupied by administrative staff. After not receiving an immediate response, the SAWS students began marching off stage in lockstep, again chanting, "No Nazis, No KKK, No TPUSA," as they proceeded to enter the crowd. They subsequently began to harass known conservative and Turning Point USA-affiliated students, screaming and spitting on us, demanding we leave the event and our university. Eventually, we ironically left the event, out of fear for our safety—*at an event advertised as* "no place for hate!" Not *once* did an administrator or faculty member—of which there were dozens present—cut the microphone or talk over these students to inform them that their hateful demands or violent demeanor toward other students was unacceptable.

The great irony is, the lockstep these student activists marched in was a perfect reflection of their idea of a utopian college setting. They flat-out *demanded* CSU ban conservative organizations from "their campus" and from "their education," insinuating that their demands extend to certain students in their classrooms simply because of their status as conservatives (which, I knew by this point, was synonymous with the term "white supremacist" to these students). They not only expected the university to march in lockstep with them but that every individual on our campus should *think* in lockstep. They claimed to be acting out of "love" to create an "inclusive, equitable, and safe education for everyone." But what was hidden between the lines of their aggressive speech was a demand that everyone on our Colorado campus look different but think exactly the same so as not to "encourage white supremacy."

It didn't matter that throughout every step of our chapter's founding and presence on campus, all Turning Point USA chapter members fiercely denounced any form of racism.

It didn't matter that our presence at the CSUnite event was peaceful, as we stood in solidarity with our community against racism (even while SAWS' angry rhetoric manifested into violent behavior toward conservative students).

It didn't even matter that most of the students involved in Students Against White Supremacy were themselves ironically, white, while our Turning Point USA chapter boasted racial and ethnic diversity—from blacks to native Cubans to everything in between.

All that mattered was that we as an organization identified as the ugly, dirty C-word: *conservative*, and the hatred toward students on our campus became warranted.

The worst part of the event? Shortly after these students concluded their diatribe of abhorrent hyperbole demanding the dismantling of Turning Point USA, the audience cheered.

Looking through the crowd, I recognized dozens of students and faculty members, with whom I had interacted and had positive relationships with joining in on the ovation. My heart sank.

Thanks to my status as the sitting Speaker in student government, I had a meeting scheduled with high-ranking faculty for the following week. Ordinarily, this meeting was designed for two other members of ASCSU and me to inform the administration of what was happening at the student level.

I cut right to the chase.

Face-to-face, I informed the top members of CSU's administration that for the prior few days, I had felt a previously unmatched sense of displacement from the university community—that I didn't truly belong here. I felt targeted, harassed, and physically unsafe walking to my classes and sitting through each lecture, and I knew dozens of other students felt the same way. Their response? They felt terrible I endured such targeted harassment, but they didn't want to "add to the cause" of SAWS' mission by cutting off their speech during the CSUnite event. They would continue to meet with SAWS representatives to create a more inclusive community. In other words, "Thanks for letting us know; we'll work on it by chatting with the people who are harassing you about how *they* feel." This initial response was heartbreaking. It further solidified my understanding that, for the most part, university administrations have a steadfast commitment to improving the college experience for leftist students but fail to invest the same level of energy and dedication toward conservative students.

Thankfully, CSU did hold up their commitment toward freedom of speech and the right for conservative students and organizations to share their values, despite the disheartening conversation I had. In the fall of 2019, leading up to Dennis Prager's successful campus visit, the CSU administration launched a free-speech initiative involving a major section of the university website. They even hosted educational seminars for the community to discuss the university's commitment to upholding the First Amendment. They certainly did not have to take this major step in the right direction, but they did, and for that, I am incredibly grateful. This small victory reinforced the truth that there were individuals in my university community, particularly in the administration, fighting for the voices of all students. I only wished we had arrived at that point much sooner and avoided the SAWS-CSUnite controversy altogether. Importantly, however, codifying free speech on our campus failed to extinguish the increasingly hostile culture toward conservative students, which had been carefully cultivated by SAWS. The university had managed to change policy, but it didn't impact student practice.

CDS spread throughout the CSU student body in 2018, my Junior year. This was embodied in the flesh via the SAWS (Students Against White Supremacy) and their attempts to divide our community. Today, I have yet to encounter any person as deeply passionate about their leftist cause as the SAWS students. By the grace of God, many cases of the CDS disease have been cured, thanks to logic and sound reasoning presented by brave conservative students on our campus. In many cases, however, the Left continues to come unglued.

The extreme hysteria reacting to the success of conservative students and organizations is not localized to the CSU campus or even to college campuses in general. Today, in the world outside the campus, conservatives are just as targeted. Right-wing commentators and public figures are frequently banned from online public forums like Facebook and Twitter; PragerU has recently been censored on multiple platforms for its videos because they are "inappropriate" and contain "nudity"—which is the farthest thing from the truth.[27] Steven Crowder, the clever brain behind the "Change My Mind" events I mentioned earlier, has frequently faced censorship and even demonization of his online platforms for sharing conservative content.[28] Donald Trump, Jr., son of President Trump and fan-favorite among young conservatives online and during campus speeches, has shared he receives the second-highest number of death threats in the nation behind his father.[29] Even those who simply desire to question the lockstep of the Left take a punch—just look at journalist Andy Ngo, who was violently attacked by Antifa members in Portland after probing the rationale for their cause, causing a brain injury. Andy spent significant time recovering in the hospital.[30]

27 Rachel del Guidice, "Google Defends YouTube Restrictions on PragerU's Educational Videos in Federal Court," *The Daily Signal*, last modified August 27, 2019, https://www.dailysignal.com/2019/08/27/google-defends-youtube-restrictions-on-pragerus-educational-videos-in-federal-court/.

28 Nick Bastone, "YouTube Says It Has Suspended the Ability of a Star with Millions of Fans to Make Money from His Videos, Following a Huge Backlash," *Business Insider*, last modified June 5, 2019, https://www.businessinsider.com/steven-crowder-youtube-channel-demonetized-2019-6.

29 Paul Bedard, "Secret Service: President Trump and Donald Trump Jr. No. 1 and No. 2 Highest Death Threats," *Washington Examiner*, last modified November 3, 2019, https://www.washingtonexaminer.com/washington-secrets/secret-service-president-trump-son-don-jr-no-1-no-2-highest-death-threats.

30 Tess Bonn, "Conservative Journalist Andy Ngo Says Assault Involving Antifa Resulted in Brain Injury," *The Hill*, last modified July 25, 2019, https://thehill.com/hilltv/rising/454712-conservative-journalist-andy-ngo-says-antifa-attack-resulted-in-brain-injury.

There are countless other examples of the Left coming unglued.

As a Biomedical Scientist, I can only prescribe one anecdote to the maniacal meltdowns of the Left: conservatives must keep getting up and fighting. It may seem difficult, dangerous, and draining, but to codify a commitment to intellectual diversity and a conservative presence on your college campus, you cannot allow the Left's tactics to scare you into silence. At CSU, thanks to a small handful of students who refused to stay silent, progress has been made. It's possible for conservatives elsewhere to reclaim their right to the college experience, too. My best advice, based on my own experiences? Adorn your boxing gloves—you're in for a fight.

CHAPTER TEN

· · · · · · · · · · · · · · · · ·

THE LIBERAL CASE FOR A CONSERVATIVE PRESENCE ON CAMPUS

"If being liberal means participating in 'cancel culture'—simply denying, ignoring, and canceling something controversial—rather than 'conversation culture,' which means having conversations and diverse dialogue, then I am comfortable saying I would rather sway to the right."

—CSU STUDENT JOURNALIST

The constant hysteria and meltdowns of leftists on campus are comical for some, and for others, draining. Often, however, it's more than that—it's enlightening, becoming a window through which to view the future of the left side of the aisle. This future is grim, more closely resembling an Orwellian 1984-esque socialist reality than the inspiring American history of our nation.

The perfect manifestation of this reality was brought to light at CSU in the fall of 2018. In the introduction to this book, I mentioned a comical news cycle, which discussed the phrase "long time no see" and how these trivial words had been deemed as offensive on the CSU campus. The story originally broke through an opinion piece in *The Rocky Mountain Collegian*, the CSU student newspaper entitled, "CSU has gone too far with inclusive language."[31] The piece was written by a liberal undergraduate student who, despite her leanings toward the left side of the aisle, concluded our university's commitment to enforcing inclusive language had crossed the line. Her experience as a first-year (not "freshman"—that's too offensive!) student involved being taught the terms "you guys" and "freshman" were exclusive to female and nonbinary students. The female author had never felt excluded or offended by someone's use of these terms. She wrote that without even asking students how they felt about certain words or phrases, the university was determining common everyday phrases to be offensive and in violation of the school's principles of community.

Deciding to investigate the concept further, the author scheduled an appointment with the ASCSU director of diversity and inclusion to discover how student government officials responded to the "inclusive language" crusade. During her meeting, the director handed her a thick packet of words and phrases that had been deemed non-inclusive by the "Inclusive Communications Task Force," an ambiguous committee organized by—no surprise—the administration's vice president for diversity and inclusion.

Shocked, the author of the op-ed wrote:

---

31   Katrina Leibee, "Leibee: CSU Has Gone Too Far with Inclusive Language," *The Rocky Mountain Collegian*, last modified November 4, 2018, https://collegian.com/2018/11/leibee-csu-has-gone-too-far-with-inclusive-language/.

"A countless amount of words and phrases have been marked with a big, red X and defined as non-inclusive. It has gotten to the point where students should carry around a dictionary of words they cannot say...we have been asked to phase out phrases from our language that we hear every day outside of this campus. However, we were never asked if we felt these terms were not inclusive, we were told."[32]

Throughout my three prior years at CSU, I had never read a more compelling piece in our student newspaper—particularly from a student who openly identified herself as leaning to the left. She narrated a concept I had never consciously stopped to consider. Our universities are deeming what is or is not right, moral, or acceptable without ever stopping to consider what students have to say. College students weren't being treated as equal voices, or even as equal adults, in the concept of our educational experience. Instead, we were being "told" what to think, believe, and value. The op-ed author's inquisitive and thoughtful narrative led me to pursue my own investigation—I was hell-bent on finding the ambiguous "packet" she mentioned in her article, and I didn't have to look hard.

One Google search revealed CSU's "Inclusive Language Guide,"[33] described as a living document that is always evolving alongside the ever-changing notion of inclusive language. Prior to the list of offensive words or phrases, the Inclusive Communications Task Force thoughtfully includes the following statement:

---

32 Ibid.

33 "Inclusive Language Guide: Living Document—Updates Made Frequently," *The Rocky Mountain Collegian*, last modified October 30, 2018, https://collegian.com/wp-content/uploads/2018/11/Inclusive-Language-Guide_10_30_18.pdf.

"The guide is not about political correctness or policing grammar, but rather helping communicators practice inclusive language and helping everyone on our campus feel welcomed, respected, and valued."

Give me a break—suggesting certain words or phrases are offensive and non-inclusive and that students are evil if they use them *isn't* about policing grammar? After my experience in the admissions office being reprimanded for the phrase "you guys," I knew this to be false.

Nonetheless, the language guide is described as "not an official policy or required practice," but implies that if you fail to abide by the suggested language, you are directly failing to contribute to the "inclusive" nature of the campus. For your reading pleasure, not to mention to shock you with how far college administrators are willing to go in the name of diversity and inclusion, I decided to include the most truly absurd statements made in the guide.

So, without further ado, buckle your seat belts for the next few minutes of insanity, taken verbatim from the guide itself.

WORD/PHRASE TO AVOID	WORD/PHRASE MEANING OR REASON PHRASE SHOULD BE AVOIDED	SUGGESTION FOR REPLACEMENT
Addicted/Like Crack	Oftentimes used to describe something that the person uses often, "I'm addicted to Netflix" or "These candies are like crack." While addicted can be appropriate in some situations, it can also cause harm to those who are truly experiencing drug addiction or are in recovery, or have friends/relatives who have experienced addiction.	I'm hooked/I'm a devoted fan of Delicious/excellent
American/America	The Americas encompass a lot more than the United States. There is South America, Central America, Mexico, Canada, and the Caribbean just to name a few of 42 countries in total. That's why the word "americano" in Spanish can refer to anything on the American continent. Yet, when we talk about "Americans" in the United States, we're usually just referring to people from the United States. This erases other cultures and depicts the United States as the dominant American country.	US citizen; person from the US.
Birth Defect	Generalizes the population and minimizes personhood, which should be acknowledged first (often called people-first language); The word "defect" implies a person is sub-par or somehow incomplete.	Person with a congenital disability or person with a birth anomaly
The Blind/The Deaf/ Eye for an Eye	Generalizes the population and minimizes personhood, which should be acknowledged first (often called people-first language). In addition, using phrases that associate blindness or deafness as negative ("an eye for an eye") can be problematic for folks with these disabilities. Some people may identify with and prefer terms like deaf and blind so it is important to ask preference.	Person who is blind, or Person who is deaf or hard of hearing

WORD/PHRASE TO AVOID	WORD/PHRASE MEANING OR REASON PHRASE SHOULD BE AVOIDED	SUGGESTION FOR REPLACEMENT
Cake Walk/Takes the cake	Slaves would covertly mock White slave owners through exaggerated dance to mimic White aristocrats. Perhaps unaware of the subversive origin of the dancing, slave owners began holding "balls" for entertainment, where slaves would perform these dances to win a cake. Cakewalks became popular through the racism of 19th century minstrel shows, which portrayed Black people as clumsily aspiring to be and dance like White people.	That was easy
Dumb/Mute	The word dumb or mute was once widely used to describe a person who could not speak and implied the person was incapable of expressing themselves. Deaf-mute was used to refer to people who could neither speak or hear. People living with speech and hearing disabilities are capable of expressing themselves in many other ways including writing and sign language.	Person who cannot speak, has difficulty speaking, uses synthetic speech, is nonvocal or nonverbal
Eenie meenie miney moe	The original song replaces Tiger with an offensive word aimed at African-Americans.	Randomly selected
Epileptic	Generalizes the population and minimizes personhood, which should be acknowledged first (often called people-first language).	Person with epilepsy, person with seizure disorder
Freshman	Using "man" terms excludes women and non-binary gender identities. Inclusive language acknowledges that people with many different identities can fill the role and can contribute.	First-year
Handicapped/ Disabled/Crippled/ Suffers from, Afflicted with, Victim of/Invalid/ Lame/ Deformed Handicap parking	These terms generalize the population and minimize personhood, which should be acknowledged first (often called people-first language); they also imply that people with disabilities are not capable.	Person with a disability/people with disabilities, uses leg braces, etc. Accessible parking, parking for people with disabilities

WORD/PHRASE TO AVOID	WORD/PHRASE MEANING OR REASON PHRASE SHOULD BE AVOIDED	SUGGESTION FOR REPLACEMENT
He or She Ladies and Gentlemen	These terms imply that gender is binary (i.e. either man or woman) and does not acknowledge that people may identify anywhere along the gender spectrum and/or their biological sex may not match their gender identity. Inclusive language ensures that all people in a room or at an event are acknowledged.	Everyone, students, Rams, people They/them/theirs/Ze/hir/ Person's name
Hip hooray!	"Hip-hip hooray" developed from the German "hep," (which was a harmless, adorable call shepherds would use when herding their sheep). But during the Holocaust, German citizens started using it as a rallying cry when they would hunt down the Jewish citizens who were living in the ghettos. And the phrase's anti-Semitic undertones go as far back as 1819, with the Hep riots—a time of both Jewish emancipation from the German Confederation and communal violence against German Jews.	Hooray
Hispanic	Widely used term to describe individuals from Spanish-speaking countries. It is problematic because of its origins in colonialization and the implication that to be Hispanic or Latinx/Latine/Latino, one needs to be Spanish-speaking. It is also problematic when people are called Hispanic based on their name or appearance without first checking to see how they identify.	Latinx/Latine/Latino Using person's country of origin such as Cuban-American
Hold Down the Fort/ Defend the Fort	In the U.S. the historical connotation refers to guarding against Native American "intruders" and feeds into the stereotype of "savages".	Cover the office/ left in charge
Homosexual	Because of the clinical history of the word "homosexual," it is used in an offensive way to suggest that gay people are somehow not "normal" or psychologically/emotionally disordered— notions discredited by the American Psychological Association and the American Psychiatric Association in the 1970s.	Gay/Lesbian/ Bisexual/ Pansexual/Queer It is important to ask what term a person prefers and not assign arbitrarily

WORD/PHRASE TO AVOID	WORD/PHRASE MEANING OR REASON PHRASE SHOULD BE AVOIDED	SUGGESTION FOR REPLACEMENT
Illegal immigrant/alien	The term "illegal immigrant" was first used in 1939 as a slur toward Jews who were fleeing the Nazis and entered Palestine without authorization. Saying that a person is "illegal" dehumanizes them and implies that they are a criminal, not taking into account that they may be a refugee seeking asylum. The term also suggests that the individual, and not the potential actions they have taken, are unlawful.	Born in [insert country], immigrant/ undocumented immigrant/refugee, if a person has been forced to leave their country to escape war, persecution, or natural disaster
Long Time No See	Originally mocking Native Americans or Chinese pidgin English.	I haven't seen you in a long time.
Man the Booth/ Mankind/ Manmade You Guys Policeman/Fireman/ Chairman	Using "man" terms excludes women and non-binary gender identities and overlooks their contributions and roles in society. Inclusive language acknowledges that people with many different identities can fill the role and can contribute.	Staff the Booth, humankind, human made or made by hand Police officer, fire fighter, chairperson, etc. Friends/colleagues/ everyone/all /folks
Male/Female	Male and female refers to biological sex and not gender. In terms of communication methods (articles, social media, etc.), we very rarely need to identify or know a person's biological sex and more often are referring to gender. In these cases, using gender identity terms is preferred.	Man/Woman/ Gender Non-Binary/Gender Non-Conforming
Mr./Mrs./Ms.	While generally acceptable, using titles can be problematic when you are not aware of a person's gender identity and try to guess or when the use of the title is against a person's personal preference. These terms also exclude folks outside of the man/woman binary. When possible, and when it is not a personal preference to use one of these titles, refer to folks by first or last name. Mx is a gender-neutral title that can also be used.	First or last name/ Mx/If they are a Dr., use that title
No Can Do	Originally a way to mock Chinese people.	I can't do it.

WORD/PHRASE TO AVOID	WORD/PHRASE MEANING OR REASON PHRASE SHOULD BE AVOIDED	SUGGESTION FOR REPLACEMENT
Paraplegic/ Quadriplegic	These terms can generalize the population and minimize personhood, which should be acknowledged first (often called people-first language); some people may identify with these terms so it is important to ask preference.	Person with a spinal cord injury, person with paraplegia, person who is paralyzed
Peanut Gallery	This phrase intends to reference hecklers or critics, usually ill-informed ones. In reality, the "peanut gallery" names a section in theaters, usually the cheapest and worst, where many Black people sat during the era of Vaudeville.	Crowd, Audience
"Preferred" Pronouns	Using the word "preferred" in front of pronouns suggests that gender identity, especially outside of the binary, is a choice and that the pronouns don't really belong to the person, they are just "preferring" them over their "true" pronouns.	Pronouns What pronouns do you use?
Rule of Thumb	The 'rule of thumb' has been said to derive from the belief that English law allowed a man to beat his wife with a stick so long as it is was no thicker than his thumb.	Standard or general rule
Starving/I'm Starving/I'm Broke	When used in place of simple saying "I'm hungry" or "I'm low on cash right now," these terms appropriate real situations of hardship and can cause harm to individuals who are experiencing extreme poverty or hunger crisis.	I'm hungry I'm low on cash
Straight	When used to describe heterosexuals, the term straight implies that anyone LGBT is "crooked" or not normal.	Heterosexual

WORD/PHRASE TO AVOID	WORD/PHRASE MEANING OR REASON PHRASE SHOULD BE AVOIDED	SUGGESTION FOR REPLACEMENT
The Grandfather Clause/ Grandfathered In	Originated in the American South, way back in the 1890s. At that time, several Southern states developed and enforced the clause as a way to defy the 15th Amendment, and thus prevent Black Americans from utilizing their then-newfound right to vote. The "grandfather clause" stated that Black men could only vote if their parents or grandparents were able to vote before the year 1867—which was, conveniently for the White supremist lawmakers, many years before Black Americans were permitted access to voting rights.	Exempt from the new rule
The itis/Food Coma	More commonly known now as a "food coma," this phrase directly alludes to the stereotype of laziness associated with African-Americans. It stems from a longer (and incredibly offensive) version. Modern vernacular dropped the racial slur, leaving a faux-scientific diagnosis for the tired feeling you get after eating way too much food.	I ate too much
Uppity	During segregation, Southerners used "uppity" to describe African-Americans who didn't know their socioeconomic place. Originally, the term started within the Black community, but White supremist adopted it pretty quickly.	Snotty or stuck up
War/Go to War/At War/War Zone/Battle	When used to describe actual war, these terms are appropriate. Otherwise, when used to describe difficult situations or meetings ("I have to go to war today at this meeting"), they evoke very real tragedy that can be problematic for survivors of war or Veterans.	Hostile environment Toxic/difficult/ confrontation/ dispute Get after it/Go get em

You honestly can't make this stuff up.

At first, I planned on choosing five to ten examples from this list, but I truly couldn't decide which words or phrases to leave off—they're all too good! I wish I could say I was clever enough to draft a list as truly hysterical as this one, even in a satirical sense. You must give the authors of the guide credit for creativity. The diversity administrators at my university truly and honestly believe the word "homosexual" (a scientific word describing someone being attracted to the same sex: "homo" meaning same and "sexual" meaning sex) is highly offensive but suggests replacing the word "straight," which is apparently also offensive, with the opposite of homosexual—heterosexual? Since when did scientific medical diagnoses like "epileptic" or "quadriplegic"—both terms I learned in my advanced neuroanatomy course—become offensive? (It's a medical diagnosis!) And hang on just one minute—you claim gender pronouns are fluid and can constantly be changing, but it's evil for me to ask what the *preferred* pronouns of the day are?! My personal favorite phrase on the list is "food coma," a term I frequently use to describe my occasional In-N-Out Burger, Chick-fil-A, or Texas Roadhouse experiences—but I better stop saying it, or I'll be a blatant racist!

Most abhorrently, the term "America" or "American" had now been deemed non-inclusive or even offensive? At this, I cringed. The other terms were shocking but comical. This, however, was inexcusable. Earlier in my college career, while flying to attend the aforementioned AAUW women's conference in Washington, DC, I sat next to a middle-aged woman with no luggage or bags. Somberly, she was simply holding a bouquet of flowers. As we approached Ronald Reagan

National Airport, she asked me what I would be doing in Washington. She shared that she would be flying back out to Denver a few hours later—she had flown for many hours on Memorial Day to quietly and humbly bring a bouquet of flowers to her late son's grave at Arlington National Cemetery. This moment was awe-inspiring and devastatingly beautiful. I held back tears as I thanked her for her continued sacrifice for our nation and dedication to those who fight for American values.

Now, however, on my college campus, referring to anyone as an American—including this woman's son and his family, who together have paid the ultimate price in the name of freedom—was *offensive*? I had never witnessed a university go so far in the name of social justice and supposed inclusivity until this moment, but CSU had certainly crossed the line.

Through this document, the CSU administration strongly implied that it is immoral to suggest that the United States of America is a superior nation to others or that any nation is superior to another. This is wrong, and objectively speaking, is a lie. *Of course* some nations are superior, particularly morally superior, to others. Free nations uphold human rights, while nations with socialist, corrupt, dictatorial governments who fail to do so are wrought with wars, starvation, refugee crises, and genocide. No American university, which boasts privileges to freedom of speech, freedom from government intervention, and freedom of religion (to name a small handful of our many liberties), can even begin to make a coherent argument that we live in a morally equal nation to those propagating human rights atrocities.

The Syrian Assad regime is actively using chemical weapons against its own civilians.[34] Chinese government officials are re-writing the Bible and the Quran to reflect socialist values and placing ethnic minorities in "re-education" camps.[35] Iranian and Russian officials are providing arms to the Syrian government to kill innocent people.[36] Unmitigated terrorist groups in Africa (such as Boko Haram) continue to wreak havoc, thanks to corrupt government officials too concerned with retaining power to control terrorism. Now, because perhaps someone was offended by one statement uttered by another free individual, American culture is no longer morally superior to the aforementioned? Seriously?! Only on an American college campus could such an egregious narrative be told.

The result of such a dangerous lie is that the next generation of Americans—those tasked with upholding the beacon to freedom shone around the world—are covering their eyes and turning away from blatant global human rights abuses. We are becoming complacent, failing to uphold the dignity of human life, because we are unaware that big government regimes do actually oppress millions of individuals. For a peaceful world to reign, this lie cannot stand.

34 Clare Lombardo, "More Than 300 Chemical Attacks Launched During Syrian Civil War, Study Says," *NPR*, last modified February 17, 2019, https://www.npr.org/2019/02/17/695545252/more-than-300-chemical-attacks-launched-during-syrian-civil-war-study-says.

35 Ryan Fahey, "China Will Rewrite the Bible and the Quran to 'Reflect Socialist Values' Amid Crackdown on Muslim Uighur Minority," *Daily Mail*, last modified December 26, 2019, https://www.dailymail.co.uk/news/article-7824541/China-rewrite-Bible-Quran-reflect-socialist-values.html.

36 Tom O'Connor, "Russia and Iran Get Closer on Security and Syria After U.S. Vote to Punish Them," *Newsweek*, last modified December 18, 2019, https://www.newsweek.com/russia-iran-ties-syria-sanctions-vote-1478031.

I was shocked after stumbling upon this document—and I continue to be. After graduation, I decided to share the insanity of CSU's Language Guide in a short, comical video. Overnight, the conservative movement lit up. Conservative media outlets from *The Blaze* to *The Daily Wire* who had covered the guide early in my senior year, published new pieces. The College Fix went so far as to state, "If Frank [President of Colorado State University] wants to champion free speech, he should rip the guide up and throw it in the garbage bin, where it belongs."[37]

Major commentators and policy leaders took to Twitter to call out CSU's condemnation of the word America, including Republican National Committee Chairwoman Ronna McDaniel, and Republican Congressman Doug Lamborn, who tagged the President of the United States!

Rep. Doug Lamborn ✔ @RepDLamborn · Jul 18, 2019
Wow! @ColoradoStateU's Inclusive Coms Task Force decided that America is a word so "offensive" it should not be spoken. I'm #ProudtobeanAmerican. All Americans from all walks of life should be able to say they're proud of their country. #ColoradoStateUniversity @realDonaldTrump

💬 106   ↻ 92   ♡ 133   ⬆

37 Jennifer Kabbany, "Here's the Truth about Colorado State University's Inclusive Language Guide," *The College Fix*, last modified August 5, 2019, https://www.thecollegefix.com/heres-the-truth-about-colorado-state-universitys-inclusive-language-guide/.

Ronna McDaniel ✔ @GOPChairwoman · Jul 22, 2019 ∨

This is pure unpatriotic insanity.

Deeply disturbing that Colorado State University is telling students to avoid using the words "America" and "American."

We should encourage ALL young Americans to be proud patriots!

'America' and 'American' Listed Among Words to Avoid at Colorado Sta...
Colorado State University has included the words "American" and "America" on its list of language to avoid because they are not ...
🔗 townhall.com

💬 2.1K   ⟲ 5.3K   ♡ 10.2K   ⬆️

Apparently, my video highlighting the guide caused a social media stir. Denver-based publications began reaching out, asking for interviews and quotes regarding the language guide, which I was happy to provide. I was filled with hope, knowing my decision to share the truth in just a few minutes through a video had drawn national attention to a subject I had been frustrated about for months. I knew even after graduating from CSU, there would be a direct impact from my decision to stand up for conservative values; if I was willing to tell the truth in the face of injustice, I could make a difference in the "real world" post-graduation.

Naturally, the CSU administration responded to the media frenzy in a hurry. The university's president and chancellor, who had been a mentor to me throughout my college experience and had written recommendation letters on my behalf for internships and graduate school, instantly countered my statements about this guide being used to silence students. In an official statement drafted by CSU's president, he stated the guide was not official university policy and was never intended to be used by students. CSU also claimed a version of the guide was "leaked" to online publications and to social media through my video as if this had been a top-secret document under lock and key.[38]

I knew his statements were false—students, who were friends of mine, working as resident assistants, had been handed the guide as a printed-out document. Further, after I left my job in the admissions office, my coworkers informed me that this guide had become part of the training for new admissions ambassadors as well. Also, at least one student government leader in ASCSU, who had been interviewed about the guide in the first place, had been tasked with helping to distribute the document. Whether the language guide was intended to be used by students or not, it was certainly influencing the student experience at CSU.

Moreover, the language guide had been publicly posted online through a hyperlink in the op-ed I first discussed in this chapter for nearly a *year* before I posted my video. If anyone chose to Google search the term "Colorado State Language Guide," the document appeared as the first search result. To claim that I had nefariously "leaked" a secret doc-

38 Sonia Gutierrez, "CSU: Current Inclusive Language Guide Does Not Discourage Use of 'America,' 'American'," *9News*, last modified July 18, 2019, https://www.9news.com/article/ news/local/next/csu-current-inclusive-language-guide-does-not-discourage-use-of-america-american/73-234acc31-6031-4a7c-87b3-e5515f07e74f.

ument was a baseless accusation aimed at discrediting me for sharing truth.

Upon reading the response from the university, I couldn't help but smile. Leaders in the administration clearly knew they had done something wrong—their contradictory statements that the guide wasn't accurate but that it also existed among faculty members was proof of that. (By the way, even if the guide *had* only been distributed among faculty members to encourage them to adhere to it, wouldn't that be bad enough?!) Once again, "that Turning Point girl" had drawn attention to the blatant leftist bias within the CSU administration, this time on the national stage.

Discovering the full Inclusive language guide was a shocking, albeit hilarious experience. With a quite liberal estimate, I suppose that approximately less than 5 percent of the student body (mostly those who worked in Residence Life and Admissions, according to my close friends) had even seen the guide with their own two eyes, let alone discussed how their language ought to be changing to create a more inclusive community environment. Yet, allegedly, offensive language had become such a clear and present problem on our campus that it warranted the creation of an entire Inclusive Communications Task Force, made up of faculty and administrative officials throughout the university. Annually, thousands of student fee and tuition dollars contributed to programs and task forces like this one, yet these committees and events likely weren't even responding to real problems happening on campus—just theoretical ones that could potentially, perhaps be offensive to some student somewhere on campus. The administration had gone too far—even raising the eyebrows of an outspoken liberal columnist in the student newspaper. This wasn't promoting inclusivity. Instead, it was telling students *what* they should be thinking, instead of teaching them *how* to think. And *that* is the crux of the matter.

The author of the op-ed later came out with an additional piece in the *Collegian*, sharing her experience after writing her thoughts on inclusive language.[39] She shared that CSU faculty members and students involved in ASCSU had attempted to pressure her to take down the article due to its popularity among national, conservative news sources like *The Blaze*. Some people in student government had proceeded to tell her that she was "not a good candidate to participate in diversity and inclusion within their organization," something she had previously been interested in pursuing. The author shared, "They brought my character into question simply because I had a different opinion."[40]

The piece shared how the experience led the author to conclude being a student at CSU had taught her she was not as liberal as she had previously thought. Now, she believes the right side of the aisle may have more merit than she had anticipated, but perhaps may be hiding under a blanket of false narrative propagated from the Left. She wrote, "If being liberal means participating in 'cancel culture'—simply denying, ignoring, and canceling something controversial—rather than 'conversation culture,' which means having conversations and diverse dialogue, then I am comfortable saying I

---

39 Katrina Leibee, "Leibee: Coming to CSU Has Made Realize I'm Not as Liberal as I Thought
    I Was," *The Rocky Mountain Collegian*, last modified February 5, 2019, https://collegian.
    com/2019/02/leibee-coming-to-csu-has-made-realize-im-not-as-liberal-as-i-thought-i-was/.

40 Ibid.

would rather sway to the right."[41] She continued to share that her observations of the current campus environment have been incredibly hostile toward "conservatives," which, in her experience, has been used as a dirty word in Fort Collins, Colorado. She knew that students (and sometimes faculty) had protested every invited conservative speaker (i.e., Charlie, Candace, and Dennis) simply because they dared to say something the Left deemed "controversial."

This young woman had once more written a profoundly compelling argument, and in my opinion, even outdid herself compared to her previous op-ed. Apparently, exposure to both sides of the aisle forced her to reexamine her own beliefs, which were still rooted in liberalism, but by then, more frequently wandered between them.

I continued to reflect on the previous years on campus, particularly when I had been referred to as "that Turning Point girl." I realized again that many of the protesters who had so aggressively expressed their outrage at Charlie Kirk's presence on campus later came to hear what Dennis Prager had to say—perhaps out of curiosity, perhaps out of genuine distaste for the speaker. Regardless of their motives, these students and even faculty members exposed themselves to a new manner of thinking by simply attending the event.

Our administration's failure to offer programming tailored to both sides of any argument had created a leftist vacuum in students' minds. After we worked to bring conservative voices to campus, however, even the most leftist students were eager to engage, at least in some way, with conserva-

41 Ibid.

tive thought. Ironically, it took a student who was willing to do the university's job for them to provide a well-rounded college experience and a 360-degree understanding of the issues of our time.

The truth is, most college students are starving (there I go using words from the forbidden list again) for new ideas—political or otherwise. Becoming a well-rounded thinker, engaging in dialogue and debate about how to improve our world, and challenging yourself to strengthen your value system—you know, what college is really *supposed* to be all about—has become secondary on college campuses. Our nation's colleges and universities have lost sight of what they were fundamentally founded to accomplish and have failed to truly educate; rather, they indoctrinate, leaving students hungry for true education and opportunities to expand their thinking. This reality is evidenced by several factors, but particularly the unbelievable turnout of students from all political backgrounds at events hosted by conservative speakers, such as Dennis Prager's speech at CSU. Quite literally, hundreds of universities across the nation could say the same (Turning Point USA alone has a presence at over 2,000 universities and hosts campus events reaching tens of thousands of students every year).

Ensuring a sense of healthy dissent in your personal life is necessary and healthy. Personally, I'm happy to have developed friendships across the aisle with inspiring young adults who challenge my values and political beliefs yet respect me. Some of my friends disagree with me on virtually every issue, but they patiently listen to my reasoning. Likewise, I am eager to hear their point of view. I never feel attacked or disrespected during our conversations; rather, I feel empowered to investigate why I believe what I do.

These friends often share with me that they have become stronger students and better leaders as a result of our relationships; discussing our differences exposes them to different vantage points, new types of problem-solving, and critical thinking other peers or professors haven't helped develop.

I have discovered that most of the time, liberals and conservatives have the same long-term vision for improving our world—we simply disagree on the means to arrive at our common destination. Leftism, on the other hand, acts as a foil to both traditional conservatism and classical liberalism and seeks to demolish the foundation of common values we have shared for so long. Without forging such strong relationships with those on the other side of the aisle, I may have never learned these critical lessons for myself.

Interestingly, the *way* we share our opinions (with respect) often leads to more change in people than the opinions themselves. For instance, in 2019, I met up with one of my friends (whom we'll call Emily), who supported Bernie Sanders in the 2016 election; Emily has always self-identified as a socialist, and we love talking politics, often challenging each other's opinions. Never have either of us mandated that the other change their beliefs. Over dinner, Emily informed me that the manner in which I've lived my young adult life has inspired her to embrace some conservative principles, despite the fact that not once have I asked her to consider them for herself.

She shared with me that through taking responsibility for my own actions and living joyfully as a victor rather than a victim, she had discovered the true meaning of conservatism.

More astonishingly, my friend rushed to tell me that without any nudging from me, she had acted on her own volition to "binge-watch" every single PragerU video (there are over 400 five-minute PragerU videos)—and was shocked to find she agreed with most of the content. Truthfully, I was floored, and I suddenly discovered the true coexistence and exchange of conservative and liberal ideas meant so much more than maintaining a passive environment. Exposure to conservative ideas can truly change hearts, minds, and even lives.

The same is true for us all; we all benefit from a healthy flow of information, especially information that challenges our perspectives, and the best students emerge from educational environments that force them to consider the pros and cons of both sides of ideologies. Having an active conservative presence on a left-leaning college campus is not something to fear—rather, it's something to actively celebrate. I believe the political polarization that has become a hallmark of today's college experience could easily be changed if we encouraged everyone to be more open about their value systems.

Most students are craving the opportunity to learn from one another. Unfortunately, our universities have failed to reach this conclusion on their own. The burden has fallen on students to promote conversations about our political divide and bridging the seemingly ever-growing gap between us, on campus, and beyond.

Thanks to incredible friendships and a small dose of courage, I never shy away from being challenged by others on why I believe what I believe. My dream is that every college student may one day feel the same way. Truly, having an active conservative voice on campus benefits everyone, including liberal students, who deserve exposure to new ways of thinking just as much as conservative students who are submerged on the left side of the aisle each day.

CHAPTER ELEVEN

ON THE FRONT LINES

"The shift in our nation's culture has been carefully cultivated for years on the front lines of America's culture war—the heart of our college campuses."

—Isabel Brown, Western Conservative
Summit Speech, 2020

Following the Charlie, Candace, and Dennis events and the SAWS debacle, at the start of my senior year (the fall of 2018), I felt a new journey tugging at my heart. My classmates in Biomedical Sciences were anxiously awaiting their acceptances to medical school, planning gap years in the Peace Corps, or getting their EMT certifications. Yet, while we had all run the race and completed our premed track, I felt in my heart that I wasn't meant to become a physician. God was leading me in a new direction, and it was going to change my life.

I started wondering what it would mean to adjust my life plan from medical school to starting something no one around me could envision by continuing my work of conservative activism through a new venue—social media.

I wanted to create an online video series to share stories like mine. My biggest frustration throughout my journey as a campus activist had been how major news networks and political influencers spent endless hours talking about how crazy college campuses had become but seemingly focused on the short-lived insanity of protests when a conservative speaker showed up. These protests are, absolutely, nothing less than absurdity, but they're only a small glimpse of a conservative students' college experience. (Plus, most of the protests aren't affiliated with the students, speaker, or campus clubs anyway.) The vast majority of the college conservative's story was not being told. No one knew that when a conservative student invited someone like Charlie Kirk to speak on campus, that student would face dire consequences for months or even years. No one knew that these students endure death threats, doxing, failing grades on assignments, impeachment from student government, and alienation from their friends, simply because they desire to catalyze dialogue in their communities. I knew that someone needed to tell the whole story. It was time to hand the microphone to students like me, who didn't have a massive social media following or a connection at Fox News to share their everyday stories.

I'll never forget the conversation I had with my parents in my family's living room when I told them I didn't want to go to medical school and that, instead, I wanted to chart my own course in politics on social media. I told them I was changing plans, but I wasn't sure exactly what my future would look like, although I predicted a law degree in the coming years and maybe someday running for office. In the meantime, I wanted to create a job through social media.

My parents are always supportive, but their faces then were *priceless*.

They agreed that I shouldn't pursue medical school, as they could see I didn't love my science studies as much as I once had. However, they couldn't wrap their heads around what "running a video series through social media" would really mean for me. To be fair, I wasn't even sure what it would mean, but deep in my heart, I knew I should use my voice for an audience much larger than my college campus. I knew I had made a deep impact at CSU and had changed the reality for CSU's conservative students, who now had a place to call home with Turning Point USA and had the foundation to stand up for their values in the classroom. Something—God, I believe—told me I could continue making a similar impact for college students and other forgotten voices all over the country if I just took the leap.

* * *

I loathe the term "social media influencer." I cringe when I hear the words, and I avoid using that phrase at all costs. (Many people refer to themselves as influencers, but they don't know if what they are posting is influencing anyone or anything. I don't believe you can call yourself an influencer—only other people can. Anyway, I digress.) While there isn't really another word to describe what political personalities and commentators do through social media activism, I could still nearly feel my soul shriveling up when I explained to my parents that I wanted to abandon medical school plans to become a social media (cringe) influencer.

My dad laughed at this word repeatedly, which eventually caused me to join in.

Will I influence anyone's opinions or behavior, anyway, I

thought. *Is sharing visual stories of conservative students just a stupid pipe dream that only five people would watch and never share?*

I had no answers to these questions, and I knew I never would unless I gave my dream a shot.

As the spring semester progressed at CSU, I cheered on my Biomedical Sciences friends as they eagerly awaited medical school acceptance letters, took their third or fourth MCAT exam (thank the Lord I don't have to take that now), and made plans for their gap years. I, on the other hand, was busy in between classes writing proposals and business plans for the first time in my life—skills they don't exactly teach you in chemistry class—and sending them to notable conservative organizations, simply asking for a shot.

It was certainly an unusual approach. Typically, you apply for a job that already exists instead of asking organizations to create an entirely new position based on a loose concept you have. For a few months, I heard nothing. Waiting was unbelievably trying. God had called my heart in a new direction, and I was sure it would work. *Surely, my dream will manifest into something,* I thought. My mind would ricochet a few moments later with the opposite thought: *maybe this is just an empty pipe dream, Isabel.*

Then, April hit, and my phone rang.

One of the most successful and notable conservative organizations in the world—PragerU—wanted to offer me a job. Me! Someone with no experience in video production received an offer from an organization who, at that point, had amassed over one billion views on their videos. Along with filming their existing videos, PragerU wanted to give my video series idea a shot. I was ecstatic, but I stood still for just long enough to hear that my plans for the next month would be changing. I would need to postpone my big move to Washington, DC for graduate school until August because I would spend the summer living in Los Angeles, California, working out of the PragerU headquarters.

My head was spinning. It was time for me to make my own video series.

* * *

That summer, my first day on the job offered filming opportunities with PragerU's CEO, Marissa Streit. I quickly learned the ins and outs of green screens, lavalier microphones, and Adobe Premiere. Within the first month, I filmed many videos and learned infinitely more than I could have on my own. We visited campuses, interviewed college students, and dove headfirst into understanding the growing culture war at our nation's universities. My employer offered me the chance of a lifetime to address the behind-the-scenes stories on college campuses that the mainstream media had failed to address, and it was working. Hundreds of thousands of people were watching the videos we were posting, and the comments kept pouring in.

In the introduction to this book, I wrote that conservative college students are the intellectual soldiers for the culture war raging across our nation. Our college campuses have become the front lines of this battle, where tolerance for intellectual diversity has plummeted, and honest debate has gone out the window. I knew this at the time, and I wanted to convey all this through my video series, which I named *On The Front Lines*.

The series would be the first of its kind, where I'd highlight an individual conservative student who was facing a similar controversy to the ones that my friends and I had faced. I would travel to the student's university to interview them, and we'd film in the heart of their campus. I wanted every viewer to know exactly where we were sitting, so students, alumni, and donors could recognize the harsh reality of intolerance toward conservative values at their school as people yelled at us or protested us during the discussion. Most of all, I wanted to expose that intolerance was happening across the country, not just at coastal schools in leftist cities. After all, extreme backlash had faced me in an agricultural western state!

For my first interview, I headed to the birthplace of the free speech movement itself, which has fundamentally transformed into an intellectual war zone for anyone who challenges the Left's lockstep—the University of California, Berkeley. I found myself sitting across from one of the strongest students I have met to date, Isabella Chow. (We talked about her in chapter three—she faced extreme controversy when she refused to sign student government legislation that violated her Catholic beliefs about transgender persons).

In 2018, Isabella's peers had introduced a piece of legislation condemning the Trump Administration's revisions to Title IX. Isabella had been elected as the senator to primarily represent the large Christian student community on her campus. Properly representing her personal values and her constituency, Isabella abstained from voting. She told me she could not, in good faith, represent the Christian community on campus by uplifting the transgender lifestyle, but she didn't want anyone to feel excluded from her campus. So, she simply abstained, essentially casting a neither yes nor no vote.

You'd think this decision wouldn't stir anyone's emotions, but you'd be dead wrong.

The week after Isabella abstained, hundreds of students and community members showed up to the weekly senate session to protest her presence in student government. They demanded that she resign and spent hours individually screaming at her, as the room quickly transformed into a sit-in as students covered every inch of floor space. Outside the meeting, various student organizations on campus had organized a massive protest to demand Isabella's removal from student government because of her allegedly "hateful" remarks and "exclusive" attitude.

I watched the video of the senate meeting, observing that through it all, Isabella quietly sat for hours, while angry leftists screamed profanities and threats in her face. She was slandered as homophobic, transphobic, and anti-LGBT. Afterward, friends escorted her to classes for months, and she told me that after this meeting, she had never walked home alone. She had become so recognizable by her fellow students that it was rare for someone not to heckle her around campus. She instantly lost all her friends in student government and was barred from the coalition of students she had run for office with in the first place because her student government "party" kicked her out.

But in that video, she sat quietly. I was amazed by her patience.

During our interview, I asked Isabella how she sat through that night with such grace. "I told them, 'I love you, God loves you, and to me, I can accept you unconditionally for who you are without promoting certain parts of how you choose to identify yourself.'"

Isabella was the perfect choice for the first *On The Front Lines* interview. She epitomized what President Ronald Reagan called a "happy warrior." She chose to love those who slandered, threatened, and isolated her, with a smile on her face, proud to promote her values and her faith. She wasn't even particularly conservative—she simply wanted there to be a place for diverse ideas and values at UC Berkeley. Like I had in my college experience, Isabella understood that it often takes a single individual willing to endure significant backlash to spark a movement welcoming like-minded individuals in the heart of a leftist campus.

The interview was done, but I still had to edit and post the video—my video, my idea. *Will anyone care?* I asked myself nervously.

Posting Isabella's episode to social media was nerve-racking. I wasn't sure people would sit through a ten-minute interview, let alone share it with those around them. But they did. Isabella's interview quickly gained hundreds of thousands of views, and thousands of people commented, thanking Isabella for her bravery. I received dozens of direct messages and emails from students like Isabella who had unique stories to share. I was euphoric—my dream to hand the microphone to courageous students without platforms had become a reality.

My second filming trip for *On The Front Lines*, this time in my home state and alma mater, was equally as gratifying. The second episode aired a few weeks after Isabella's, this time featuring Marcos, a friend of mine and student at CSU. Marcos had fled Cuban socialism and legally immigrated to the United States when he was seventeen.

Like me, the Left particularly targeted him as a member of the Turning Point USA chapter at CSU. In fact, our pals in the SAWS coalition labeled Marcos—a native Cuban with a thick accent—as a white supremacist.

Rewind.

Read that again.

As I sat down with Marcos for our interview on my old campus just over a month after graduating, my heart swelled with joy. The interview with Isabella exceeded my wildest dreams, and I jumped at the opportunity to tell the world the truth about what it was like to be a conservative at *my* school. Like Isabella, Marcos embodied the "happy warrior" spirit. We laughed through the entirety of his interview, partly at the insanity of leftism, but mostly because we were joyfully passionate to tell the truth.

Not only is Marcos a first-generation American, but he's also a first-generation college student. He shared his heartbreaking history of growing up in Cuba, and I was instantly transported back to my time in this tragically beautiful place.

He shared many stories from Cuba—from his father being targeted by the communist government for spreading the Christian gospel to the grocery rations given to each Cuban family. Marcos explained that his Cuban spirit pushed him to work hard, so as soon as he arrived in the United States, he accepted minimum wage jobs before falling in love with construction.

At the end of the interview, he shared that he would become an American citizen in a few months. He nearly fell out of his chair while sharing this news, and his excitement was contagious. I held back tears, witnessing the simple joy of the American spirit that he expressed.

Hilariously, we also discussed Marcos's encounters with SAWS on the CSU campus. At one point, he had calmly shared his values on individual freedom and limited government with a member of SAWS. Then, it was on—he was forever labeled a white supremacist. His response made me laugh.

"What do you mean I'm a white supremacist? Can't you hear my accent? I just told you I am from Cuba!"

It didn't matter to the (white, by the way) students accusing him of racism. All that mattered was his conservative ideology. The irony of white leftists who grew up in a privileged American reality labeling a native Cuban who grew up under the Castro regime as a white supremacist continues to baffle me. But this is the reality for countless minority conservative college students.

Like Isabella's episode, Marcos's interview outperformed my

expectations. Views and comments poured in, viewers asked for more episodes, and they thanked Marcos for expressing his American pride and encouraged him to continue expressing his values in the face of backlash. I was once again overwhelmed with joy to highlight someone with a compelling story. I knew it was just the beginning of *On The Front Lines*.

Throughout the summer of 2019, I interviewed many other students and documented their stories. Justine, a student at Syracuse University, was kicked out of her dorm after dressing up as First Lady Melania Trump for Halloween; RAs deemed her costume an act of intolerance. Student government prevented Joshua, grandson to survivors of communism, from starting a Turning Point USA chapter at Rider University, officially deeming the organization as racist. After student government voted to ban her university's Turning Point USA chapter from campus, Stormi, the chapter president at Texas State University, defended her organization's right to exist—she stood up to protesters in a student government meeting and worked with Texas Governor Greg Abbott to recognize ideological diversity on college campuses. Meanwhile, leftist students labeled her as a "race traitor" because she's Hispanic *and* conservative. They even offered anyone on campus money in exchange for her apartment address. Then there's Tiana, a former leftist, who transformed her life after watching PragerU videos and accepting conservative values and a Christian faith.

These stories represent a handful of the thousands of students with similar stories in our nation. Witnessing the simple joy of encouraging others with their stories continues to touch my heart.

After releasing the first two episodes of *On The Front Lines* with PragerU and filming many more, we mutually decided to part ways regarding the series (we are both happy with that decision—we simply had different ideas about the series' future). These days, I produce it on my own, which means I spend a good amount of time combing through footage, learning how to use Adobe Premiere, and filming all on my own. I am certainly no expert in video production, but I continue to learn more every day.

As summer ended and my graduate school program began at Georgetown, I moved from Los Angeles to Washington, DC, and restructured my involvement with PragerU. At the same time, I continued to grow my social media following and honed in on my voice within the conservative movement. I progressed with my graduate studies and simultaneously continued making intermittent videos with PragerU.

In the Spring of 2020, I was offered a staff role within Turning Point USA. I was asked to join the organization in a new capacity as a contributor, and today I serve as a spokesperson on national television, at major conferences, on the front lines of college campuses, and through social media. I regularly have the opportunity to share Gen Z's conservative identity on Newsmax, Fox News, Sky News, and more. I am deeply blessed that my journey with Turning Point USA did not end with college graduation but continues to shape my next chapter.

Today, I am living my American Dream. I am living proof that a single idea can manifest into a career and a livelihood. I still look back and chuckle at the tearful yet funny conversation on the couch with my parents a few months before filming my first *On The Front Lines* episode, when I explained that I would abandon the concrete plans I had made and let my heart lead the way. In a handful of months, I have grown into a stronger advocate for conservative principles than I could have ever anticipated. I have been featured on the cover of *Newsweek* magazine, sharing my support for President Trump. Millions of people have engaged with the videos I've produced for organizations like PragerU and Turning Point USA or on my own, and I am occasionally asked to take photos with high school or college students in airports or at conferences who say they want to have a job like mine. I don't share this to toot my own horn; rather, I share this to express that it was through abandoning my plans for medical school and listening to God's quiet whisper to expose the truth that I experienced unplanned success and immeasurable joy. I have fallen in love with my life all over again and have been reminded of the power of a single voice resonating with truth.

Lastly, I have discovered the value of telling the stories of others. Some people who work in the (ugh) influencer space are doing so for the wrong reasons. They desire personal fame, countless brand partnerships, and large salaries. They want their lives to look edited to perfection on side-by-side squares as you scroll through their profiles. They're in it for themselves rather than for a particular movement. What I've found, however, is the impact someone can make by not caring who the credit goes to. When your content centers around handing off the microphone and highlighting the compelling stories of other people rather than self-promotion, it speaks for itself. It is a true honor to provide a platform for those who don't have a large social media following and to narrate what a day in the life of the average conservative student activist looks like. It's not flashy, it doesn't involve lots of camera time for myself, but I know in my heart that it will make a large impact on this conservative movement we are fighting for.

I often find myself smiling while listening to speakers at large conferences or campus events as they unintentionally repeat the phrase, "on the front lines." Countless leaders in the fight for freedom, including Charlie Kirk, Donald Trump, Jr., and even President Trump have emphasized in speeches the reality of college students fighting "on the front lines" of our nation's culture war. In this way, God continues to remind me that the name for my first idea in video production rings with truth. My personal front lines continue to evolve as I graduate and move on to new opportunities and seasons of life. However, today's conservative college students are warriors in the campus battle I was proud to fight during my own collegiate experience. I will not forget their stories, and I am proud to tell them. While my battleground scenery evolves as I grow and change, I know that the best is yet to come. After all, the future of America is at stake.

CHAPTER TWELVE

POLITICS *DO* BELONG AT THE DINNER TABLE

"[Our]societal deterioration could have been prevented by a handful of lively conversations around the dinner table, not to indoctrinate beliefs from one generation to the next, but to challenge them, understand them, and expose the next generation to the art of exploration of ideas."
—OPINION PIECE BY ISABEL BROWN, WESTERN JOURNAL

If you ask most people today what two things never belong at the dinner table, they will automatically, almost robotically, answer, "politics and religion." In fact, a recent NPR survey revealed that 58 percent of Americans believe politics have no place around the dinner table.[42] Millennials and older members of Generation Z have been programmed to believe we should never confront our ideological or value-based differences, especially while ingesting food! Such a confrontation would surely destroy the relationships and

---

42 Jessica Taylor, "Americans Say to Pass the Turkey, Not the Politics, at Thanksgiving This Year," *NPR*, last modified November 21, 2017, https://www.npr.org/2017/11/21/565482714/americans-say-to-pass-the-turkey-not-the-politics-at-thanksgiving-this-year.

perhaps even the culinary experience. It's simply easier to pretend those differences aren't there or look past the most fundamental aspects of our identities.

A Reuters/Ipsos opinion poll conducted in the fall of 2017 found that in anticipation of the Thanksgiving holiday, half of respondents said that they expected not to discuss politics at dinner, while one-third planned to actively *avoid* talking about politics with friends and family. Moreover, 62 percent of respondents identified politics as one of their least favorite topics to discuss over holiday meals and gatherings.[43] What does this all mean? *Why* do we actively avoid speaking to each other about two of the most integral parts of our lives?

Simply put, our nation has forgotten how to peacefully articulate what they believe, why they believe it, and challenge these beliefs by exposing themselves to different vantage points—even among friends and family. As a result, by avoiding these crucial conversations at the dinner table, America's young adults have developed a fundamental lack of or misunderstanding of both politics and religion.

I grew up very differently. Unlike most of today's young adults, my parents raised me to engage in complex discussions about both politics and religion around the dinner table with my family. Partially, this is because my parents are religious and lawyers. Mostly, though, it's because my parents and grandparents actively exposed their children to complex political and social issues at a young age by

---

43   Chris Kahn, "One in Three U.S. Adults to Avoid Talking Politics over Holiday Season: Reuters/Ipsos Poll," *Reuters*, November 17, 2017, https://www.reuters.com/article/us-usa-holidaypolitics-poll/one-in-three-u-s-adults-to-avoid-talking-politics-over-holiday-season-reuters-ipsos-poll-idUSKBN1DH1DH.

encouraging discussion about those topics. The regularly encouraged political discourse in my family always produced debate because of partisan division and a family love of switching sides to play devil's advocate. I never felt criticized for holding views that differed from my parents' or siblings' views. If I had done the research and grasped a fundamental understanding of the issue at hand, productive discourse was encouraged, never punished.

Most importantly, there was never a "kids table" at our family gatherings or holidays with grandparents. We kids sat with the adults and engaged in adult conversation. We were given the freedom to ask anything we wanted, and we expected to learn something by the end of every meal. Perhaps some kids would call this boring, but for me, it was thrilling. I loved hearing my parents take opposite sides on an issue, debating the intricacies of a ballot initiative or something they'd heard during that year's State of the Union address. Talking politics over dinner taught me to question my world, to always identify both sides of any issue, and to always do the research before forming my own opinion.

The earliest memory I have of distinctly self-advocating my beliefs on a political issue occurred in sixth grade while attending a Montessori school (which are notoriously liberal). My teacher told me to conduct a scientific research project on the animal species of my choice. Being both a dog lover and an outdoorsy kid, I chose the coyote. At the time, my sisters and I took horseback riding lessons at a local barn a few times a week, and my horseback riding instructor offered to let me take a coyote pelt she had at the barn to school for the evening science fair, where I would present my project to students, teachers, and parents. (My instructor had found a dead coyote near the barn a few months earlier and kept the pelt.)

During my presentation, I proudly shared my research and hands-on learning experience. Unbeknownst to me, multiple parents complained, on-the-spot, about the coyote pelt: they were incredibly offended that the skin of a dead animal was present near their children (the horror!).

The principal quietly pulled my parents aside to tell them that, in the middle of the science fair, my presentation would need to be torn down, packed up, and taken home.

In the wake of what I like to call coyote-gate, my parents sat me down and asked me about the incident. I shared that being censored over a political issue, particularly by adults, did not yield a particularly open-minded learning environment for a child. I craved learning opportunities, and I came to my own conclusion: I wanted to attend a different school the following year. (I probably get some of my cheekiness from my mom. Shortly after all this, my parents attended parent-teacher meetings with my science teacher, who, during the meeting, proudly announced that his wife had been a former EPA bureaucrat, to which my mother responded, "Perhaps we've met! I'm a mining lawyer!").

Maybe I shouldn't have been put in a situation where self-advocacy was so necessary at such a young age (eleven). Regardless, because I had been raised to develop my own values and opinions, I was prepared for the situation. Something as simple as dedicating a few minutes at the dinner table to political- and value-based discussion had given me a new perspective. I wasn't responsible for the reactions of others, especially those older than myself, but I could maturely respond with a different opinion.

My family's commitment to exposing me to self-advocacy and critical thinking extended into my high school years, when my mother encouraged (cough, cough, *forced*) me to join the competitive speech and debate team. Early on, I rolled my eyes and dragged my feet on the way to every meeting and in preparation for every tournament, dreading the upcoming dozens of hours of research and practice speeches awaiting me. Nothing seemed worse to a fourteen-year-old than compiling binders with thousands of pages of research on topics like abolishing the penny, the potential economic impact of Bitcoin, or the Law of the Seas. Slowly, however, I realized the joy of understanding the complex political and social problems of our time. Thanks to the extensive research I had to compile on dozens of subjects—from raising the minimum wage to the impact of Mongolian rice exportation on the global GDP—I learned how to consider any problem from a 360-degree perspective. As I researched topics, my critical brain trained itself on how to consider both the positive and negative reactions of any particular solution. Speech and debate was a *lot* of work, but it provided excellent training in how to be a seeker of truth.

Fast-paced debate rounds and extemporaneous speaking topics forced me to advocate for my own values but also to challenge them by adopting opposing arguments. This translated to my everyday life. Political confrontation didn't intimidate me because debate taught me the art of productively discussing polarizing issues. Opposing beliefs were not something to fear, but instead, opportunities to create positive conversations to better understand the other side of an argument and broaden one's worldview.

I adopted a Renaissance perspective, taking all elements of a debate into account before landing on one side of an issue. I discovered that leaning one way or another on the political spectrum does not automatically subscribe you to check all 100 percent of "your side's" policy initiatives. Rather, politics involves more gray area than media and politicians would have us believe.

I frequently traveled the nation, competing at Ivy League tournaments and the National Speech and Debate tournament to share my unique voice and perspective. Most rewarding, I became a middle school debate coach, which allowed me to share my love of the game and commitment to critical thinking with the next generation, nearly all of whom went on to become successful high school debaters.

My extra research and passion for current events soon spilled over into other aspects of my life. I found myself eagerly raising my hand to share my opinions in class or ask questions. My classmates at my Catholic high school rolled their eyes in our religion courses when my liberal friend Elena and I would go back and forth on an issue for what seemed like hours. I listened to the news on the drive to school and started to earnestly look forward to the next presidential debate or State of the Union address. My peers would laugh at my political interest and ended up voting me to be "most likely to become president" in the senior yearbook to poke fun, but I didn't mind.

I fell in love with discourse, the political process, and critical thinking, thanks in large part to speech and debate. However, not everyone needs to join speech or debate. Conversations about social, political, or religious issues can and should start right at home, around your dinner table. Because young adults were taught to avoid these subjects with more ferocity than getting a root canal, we've all forgotten how to have conversations about virtually anything at all with someone we disagree with. In 2020, most college students don't enter college with a firm foundation in religious or political beliefs—largely because it's become taboo for people to talk about politics and religion at the dinner table (or in their family unit in general). Simply put, as an entire generation, we've lost our voice.

It's about time we get it back.

In 2018, Deloitte, one of the largest business consulting companies in the world, conducted a study entitled, "2018 Deloitte Millennial Survey: Millennials disappointed in business, unprepared for Industry 4.0."[44] The study explored millennial and Gen-Z adults and their lack of four top skills needed for the professional world. Over 10,000 millennials (those born between 1981 and 1996) and over 1,800 Gen-Zers (those born in 1997 and onward) from across thirty-six countries were surveyed. What lacking skills made the top four, you ask? Interpersonal skills and critical thinking, both of which come through exposure to dialogue and debate as children. Yet, when we teach our youth that politics and religion are taboo, we create a dependent generation incapable of articulating their values for themselves. They become unwilling to confront disagreements. They end up lacking interpersonal skills and critical thinking, just as the study showed.

---

44 "The Deloitte Millennial Survey 2018: Millennials' Confidence in Business, Loyalty to Employers Deteriorate," Deloitte, accessed September 30, 2020, https://www2.deloitte.com/tr/en/pages/about-deloitte/articles/millennialsurvey-2018.html.

And in case you were wondering, colleges and universities are not in the business of teaching these skills. Outside of a handful of studies in higher education, "critical thinking" is really a code word for "leftist thinking." Let me offer an example of this "leftist-I-mean-critical-thinking."

In the fall semester of my senior year, I needed to take a Writing Arguments course as a general education requirement, despite my many writing courses through the Honors Program. The course involved writing a single argument-based paper throughout the semester on any argument of one's choice. The goal of this course was to develop critical thinking skills with every student. My instructor from the English department was a young female professor in her late twenties who was clearly a miserable leftist. She would come to class each day slumping and complaining about one political issue or another and *loved* giving me the stink eye over the pro-Trump stickers on my laptop.

Interested in pursuing healthcare policy as a career at the time, and having been recently accepted to Georgetown to pursue a master's in Biomedical Sciences Policy and Advocacy, I chose to argue how the United States healthcare system ought to be reformed to create a stronger health system for Americans. On the second assignment of the course, students were to outline what the core arguments for their paper would be. I received an F. *Seriously, an F?* I thought. Confused, I sent an email to my professor to discuss this confusing result.

In response to my inquiry, my professor simultaneously claimed that I failed to follow her instructions on the rubric but had also plagiarized the rubric by following her instructions verbatim, inserting her prompt's questions word-for-word into my assignment. Bewildered at her lack of logic, I sat in her office silently, unsure how to respond before thanking her for her time and heading home to scratch my head for a few hours. After pondering the situation further, I sent her an email to ask about any opportunity for another look at the grade, given my effort and how closely I had followed her prompt. I received a particularly volatile email in return, claiming that I "lacked critical thinking skills" because I had simply prescribed to the set of directions she had provided instead of being more creative with how I compiled my product. Based on my many years in speech and debate, experiences interning for the federal government writing advanced policy memos, and recent acceptance into an elite graduate school, I was shocked.

Something wasn't adding up, so I took a quick trip to www. ratemyprofessors.com, a site through which students rate their experience with professors. I quickly discovered that dozens of other students had similar experiences with my professor, who had an average rating of 1.96 on a 5.0 scale—a *terrible* quality rating compared to most of her colleagues on the site. Comments left by prior students included: "Worst professor I have ever had by far. Grades based off if she likes you or not. Grading not clear at all. Doesn't even teach."; "She graded me super harshly because she did not agree with my topic, and she tried to bring her own personal life into literally every lecture."; "Terrible. Grades are linked to her mood for the day, which is usually awful. VERY unclear expectations. Rude and condescending. Loves to have the feeling of power and will not hesitate to drop a deuce on your day with her sarcastic attitude."[45] *Yikes*, I thought after scrolling through the comments.

But then, of course, everything made sense—maybe my professor didn't *really* believe my work was horrible. Maybe she loved having a feeling of power over her students and tended to give students she disagreed with failing grades without proper explanation—all under the guise of helping her students become successful "critical thinkers!" Given the extreme ratio of leftist to conservative professors on campus and the look of scorn from this professor at the stickers on my laptop, it's safe to assume my failing grade was linked to her disdain for my political values.

Situations occur like this one on college campuses every day.

Professors, particularly young twenty-somethings just starting their academic career, are more intent on developing leftist thinkers than critical thinkers. Perhaps this phenomenon is a resulting product of the leftist indoctrination they received as students, or maybe it has more to do with the types of young professors universities are hiring. Regardless, in the liberal arts fields, most colleges won't develop a student's capacity to think critically unless it leads to a leftist conclusion.

Parents, grandparents, and other mentors—*you* must expose the nation's youth to complex conversations. That burden rests on you. The consequences of failing to do so are dire—as an entire generation of college students will enter college without a firm foundation in their own value system. They

---

45   "Sharon Grindle," Rate My Professors, accessed September 30, 2020, https://www.ratemyprofessors.com/ShowRatings.jsp?tid=1526075.

will simply take everything their professors say as fact. Students who begin college as moderate liberals often progress into self-proclaimed socialists who believe a revolution is necessary to destroy our "oppressive" Western society. Many of my own friends and peers from college who began school with a set of *conservative* ideas quickly evolved into SJWs, simply because their convictions were not strong enough to withstand today's indoctrination. If I haven't yet convinced you that the growing abuse of power among leftist professors is alarming, I hope that thought certainly will.

* * *

The dinner table, surrounded by family, is the perfect place to explore differences in opinion. Family is family, after all, and unconditional love creates a space capable of exploring one's true beliefs. Thankfully, political, religious, and value-based discussions do not have to devolve into diatribes against those we disagree with. While we may not always *like* each other (siblings, can I get an "amen"?!), we will always *love* each other. Our perspective on the world typically begins and ends with our family, which makes families the perfect vehicles for developing open minds.

I attribute all my critical thinking skills, desire for discourse, and respect for other beliefs to exposure to these concepts at the dinner table with my family and other adults I looked up to. I was never discouraged from speaking about an "adult" or complex subject, regardless of my age. To the contrary, my older mentors always encouraged me to find my voice and use it to make an impact on my community and the world. This doesn't mean you must indoctrinate your children one way or another. Instead, expose your kids to new ideas. Invite them to sit at the adult table. Engage them in discourse and debate. Let them know it's okay to believe what they want if they have good reasons. If every family in America made this a priority, think of the future we'd create.

Politics *do* belong at the dinner table.

....

CHAPTER THIRTEEN

IN THE ARENA

THE FUTURE OF AMERICA'S
CULTURE WAR

"It is not the critic who counts; not the man who points out how the strong man stumbles, or where the doer of deeds could have done them better. The credit belongs to the man who is actually in the arena."

—PRESIDENT THEODORE ROOSEVELT

America's colleges and universities have transformed into perpetual battlegrounds for the future of our nation's values. This fight is more significant than most individuals comprehend, particularly if they are removed from higher education. This combative environment is not suitable to educate and equip our young adults with the tools they need to create a successful future. We need to teach young adults *how* to think, not *what* to think. Most colleges and universities focus on investing their resources into leftist indoctrination—in classrooms, in student leadership positions, and in the environments cultivated on campuses. This all leads to a declining value of the standard bachelor's degree in certain fields. For undergraduate students, higher education must be fundamentally altered if we, as a nation, are to recapture the once-essential value of obtaining a college degree.

Dennis Prager and other prominent conservative intellectuals frequently say that unless you want to become a doctor, engineer, lawyer, or enter another profession that requires an undergraduate degree, perhaps you shouldn't bother with attending a four-year university at all. I don't necessarily agree with this based on my principled belief in education. A lover of learning, I recently completed my graduate degree and hope to attend law school in the future. However, Dennis and others should cause many to pause and consider the cost-benefit analysis of receiving a college diploma.

As of February 2019, the Federal Reserve estimated that over forty-four million Americans collectively hold the burden of nearly $1.5 trillion in student debt, meaning roughly one in four American adults are currently paying off student loans.[46] In the spring of 2016, *The Wall Street Journal* reported that seven in ten college graduates borrowed money to pay for the rising cost of their undergraduate diploma, and on average, college students had an average of over $37,000 in debt—per student!—upon graduation.[47] This is a staggering figure for the average twenty-something—that amount could purchase a new car, put a down payment on a house, or finance multiple trips around the world.

---

46 "Student Loans Owned and Securitized, Outstanding," FRED Economic Data, last modified August 7, 2020, https://fred.stlouisfed.org/series/SLOAS.

47 Josh Mitchell, "Student Debt Is About to Set Another Record, But the Picture Isn't All Bad," *The Wall Street Journal*, last modified May 2, 2016, https://blogs.wsj.com/economics/2016/05/02/ student-debt-is-about-to-set-another-record-but-the-picture-isnt-all-bad/.

Mike Rowe, Host of television hit, *Dirty Jobs*, and Founder of the Mike Rowe Works Foundation, a scholarship program seeking to educate young Americans outside of the traditional college route, is passionate about the importance of trade school as an alternative to undergraduate education. His scholarship program emphasizes that throughout recent American history, our culture has placed a four-year degree on a pedestal while simultaneously stripping hands-on pathways to success—namely community colleges, trade schools, and apprenticeship programs—of any value. As a result, our nation has a massive skills gap contributing to an extreme number of unfilled, high-paying jobs that don't require four-year degrees. The Associated General Contractors of America reports 70 percent of construction companies nationwide are experiencing difficulty finding qualified workers,[48] and the Bureau of Labor Statistics has found the construction industry will create one-third of all new jobs nationwide through 2022.[49] Moreover, the US Department of Education has recently reported there will be 68 percent more job openings in infrastructure-related fields in the next five years than there are Americans currently training to fill them.[50]

As if that weren't enough, prior to the impact of COVID-19, job openings in America were at an all-time high, with

48 "Seventy-Percent of Contractors Have a Hard Time Finding Qualified Craft Workers to Hire Amid Growing Construction Demand National Survey Finds," AGC, last modified August 29, 2017, https://www.agc.org/news/2017/08/29/ seventy-percent-contractors-have-hard-time-finding-qualified-craft-workers-hire-am-0.

49 Ashley Gross and Jon Marcus, "High-Paying Trade Jobs Sit Empty, While High School Grads Line Up for University," *NPR*, last modified April 25, 2018, https://www.npr.org/sections/ed/2018/04/25/605092520/ high-paying-trade-jobs-sit-empty-while-high-school-grads-line-up-for-university.

50 "Advancing CTE in State and Local Career Pathways," Perkins Collaborative Resource Network, accessed September 30, 2020, https://cte.ed.gov/initiatives/ advancing-cte-in-state-and-local-career-pathways-system.

over seven million open positions—exceeding the number of available employees nationwide—with the vast majority found in skilled trade positions like construction, infrastructure, welding, electricity, etc.[51] According to the Georgetown Center on Education and the Workforce, in total, there are roughly forty million total jobs in the United States that pay employees an average of $55,000 per year that don't require bachelor's degrees at all.[52]

Even removing the cost-benefit analysis of attending an undergraduate university, particularly to study in a field without significant job opportunities after graduation, our nation must decide whether attending a traditional university is worth it.

Throughout my college experience and, in particular, through conducting research for this book, I have discovered that universities aren't operating like businesses. The consumers—in this case, students and parents paying tuition—have little to no say in how universities operate or educate. This disappointing truth is evident in every aspect of the higher education system in America. Student course evaluations are scrapped in the name of diversity. Students are mandated to enroll in courses focused entirely on leftism to receive their diplomas. Students collectively pay millions of dollars in tuition and student fees, which ultimately contributes to bankrolling diversity offices, leftist speakers, or conferences hosted on campus. Rarely, if ever,

---

51 Jeffry Bartash, "U.S. Job Openings Hit a Record 7.1 Million, Exceed Number of Unemployed Americans," *MarketWatch*, last modified October 16, 2018, https://www.marketwatch.com/story/us-job-openings-jump-to-record-71-million-2018-10-16.

52 The Good Jobs Project, accessed September 30, 2020, https://goodjobsdata.org/.

are students invited to participate on panels responsible for hiring campus administrators or university presidents.

Instead of work-centered studies, leftists indoctrinate their classrooms by mandating "diversity courses." But are they teaching diversity of thought, culture, or intellect? No, they're only teaching about the external diversity that allows everyone to *look* different but *think* exactly the same. These mandated diversity courses have little to do with workforce or leadership success: even the names betray this. At CSU, for example, diversity courses include "Border Crossings: People/Politics/Culture," "African-American Resistance and Self-Creation," and "Race Formation in the United States." The most frightening thing is *not* that our nation's young adults must sit through these courses of clear indoctrination in the first place. Rather, the primary issue is that these students are entering the college environment without a foundation for their values and, as such, are likely to accept the many fallacies taught by their professors in diversity classes and beyond as concrete fact.

These courses fail to expand thinking for young Americans on college campuses through education. Instead, the indoctrination woven into the curriculum forces students to think through a single lens—leftism—and encourages passionate belief in the Left's teachings.

Meanwhile, administrative officials diminish or ignore the conservative voice by actively targeting them, all in the name of inclusivity. If students from *any* political affiliation dare to speak out or even question a leftist doctrine, (like an aforementioned liberal student on my campus did with her "inclusive language" op-ed at CSU), they meet pressure to remove their commentary—or else. And yet, here's the craziest part of it all—we as a nation simply keep our heads down and go along with it, content with paying our colleges and universities thousands upon thousands of dollars without ever questioning where these dollars are going.

If students and their parents, who often subsidize the insane rising costs of higher education, choose to spend their thousands of dollars elsewhere, circumventing colleges and universities altogether, something must change. Universities would reexamine their operations and the product they offer. Perhaps mandated diversity courses would disappear from graduation requirements, social justice projects would find their financing from outside the student body, and faculty members would be strictly evaluated on how well they teach their students.

It's high time that our nation's college students and their families reclaim the value of their dollar by demanding higher quality education.

And, perhaps we should reconsider sending young adults without degree plans to college. We are saddling them with debt as universities force them to take classes (which, yes, cost money and *lots* of it!) that don't track to any professional field whatsoever. Perhaps, in some cases, we should encourage America's youth to embrace trade school or a gap year, or at least consider whether a $100,000+ bachelor's degree is truly the right choice for everyone.

Despite the rising number of my peers and mentors who advocate for circumventing the traditional four-year college, I still believe in its value—at least in fields that require a four-year degree to consequently attend graduate school in pursuit of a particular career. I am a product of public higher education at a large state university, and I completed graduate school at Georgetown in 2020, thanks to a vigorous and challenging Biomedical Sciences undergraduate program. However, I also observe that countless aspects of my undergraduate experience, inside of the classroom and out, failed to contribute to my success in graduate school, or as an adult, in any capacity. Through extreme professor bias, multiple years in student government leadership, and gaining a reputation as "that Turning Point girl," I also understand fighting in the lion's den. I know how it feels to boldly battle on the front lines to preserve conservative values. It's not easy. Conservative students who have yet to attend college and believe that a four-year degree is the best pathway to success should not be afraid, but they should know up front what kind of environment they are entering into.

* * *

Just after his presidency ended, former President Teddy Roosevelt delivered what would become one of the most famous and impassioned speeches of his life. The words artfully scripted in his "Man in the Arena" speech will remain forever enshrined in history. They are, in my opinion, some of the most awe-inspiring words ever spoken. The speech drew attention to the superfluous role of the critic condemning those who fearlessly attempt to make the world a better place. Instead, President Roosevelt's words placed glory on the shoulders of those placing themselves in the "arena":

> "It is not the critic who counts; not the man who points out how the strong man stumbles, or where the doer of deeds could

have done them better. The credit belongs to the man who is actually in the arena, whose face is marred by dust and sweat and blood; who strives valiantly; who errs, who comes short again and again, because there is no effort without error and shortcoming; but who does actually strive to do the deeds; who knows great enthusiasms, the great devotions; who spends himself in a worthy cause; who at the best knows in the end the triumph of high achievement, and who at the worst, if he fails, at least fails while daring greatly, so that his place shall never be with those cold and timid souls who neither know victory nor defeat."[53]

Despite the rising burden of student debt, the declining number of opportunities in the workforce for our nation's most educated young adults, and the direct exposure to leftist indoctrination on our nation's college campuses, I do not believe it is too late to reclaim the value of an undergraduate degree. But we must use the powerful voice of the "man in the arena." By working with Turning Point USA, in student government, and by advocating my values as an individual, I experienced the power of the man in the arena on my campus: when a single, daring individual is willing to challenge the leftist status quo, a strong ripple effect follows.

Today, my call to action, to "enter the arena" by fighting this culture war on the front lines in bold and loud ways, has evolved beyond the grounds of a college campus. After graduating, I discovered that the battle for liberty graduated with me. America's challenges today extend beyond academia and reside in the halls of Congress, in corporate boardrooms,

---

53 Michael McKinney, "Theodore Roosevelt's The Man in the Arena Speech 100th Anniversary," *Leading Blog*, last modified Aril 23, 2010, https://www.leadershipnow.com/ leadingblog/2010/04/theodore_roosevelts_the_man_in.html.

and on social media feeds. Americans across our country face the grim reality of "cancel culture" when they support conservative values. They risk their jobs, reputations, and in some extreme cases, their safety.

We've now seen the "front lines" evolve beyond the college campus to the streets of America. In recent months, the battles college students have been facing for years became evident to the world. We've seen riots, looting, burning of churches, major increases in physical violence, homicide, and perhaps the deepest sense of division in our nation since the Civil War.

Making the decision to speak up—literally, by saying something in student government—was not an easy one for me. I knew I would be risking friendships, mentorships, and respect, but I could see the potential impact of a single voice standing in truth. Today, my career is based on the continued use of my voice to advocate for conservative values. The challenges associated with that calling remain, but the stakes have gotten higher as the culture war seeps beyond our campuses and onto our city streets. Our fight is only beginning, and our nation is relying on *all* of us to proclaim our values with our unique voices. To step up to the front lines of this battle looks daunting, but our embrace of this call to action will determine America's story in the years ahead.

I don't say this because it sounds heroic and intellectual. There are now dozens, if not hundreds, of students at CSU who feel comfortable speaking up in their classes, wearing conservative-themed pins on their backpacks, or even confronting the university faculty and administration. Moreover, I personally know hundreds of students across the nation whose campuses are experiencing the same revolution—the bravest members of my generation are dedicated to reclaiming diversity of thought on their campuses, and it's starting to change higher education. The newest college students, in particular, those who are Gen-Zers like myself, are considered to be the most conservative generation in recent American history—a fact several national polls have confirmed.[54],[55] More often, thanks to the bravery of a few, students and professors alike continue to challenge the leftist indoctrination that has been blindly accepted for so long in higher education.

Speaking up against our university administrators and faculty members is a fantastic first step. However, simply speaking and standing up against the leftist pressure is not enough. We must expose the reality of what is happening behind the scenes on our college campuses and bring these realities to the light. If we want to make a true, lasting impact, we must reveal the leftist diatribes professors spew in classrooms, discover how our tuition and student fee dollars are being spent, and expose what our university administrators don't want the world to know. Only through direct exposure will America's higher education fundamentally transform. We must recover the value of a four-year diploma, insist that universities offer practical solutions and degree programs suited to our nation's needs, and stop the incessant indoctrination of our nation's young adults.

---

54 Ashley Stahl, "Why Democrats Should Be Losing Sleep Over Generation Z," *Forbes*, last modified August 11, 2017, https://www.forbes.com/sites/ashleystahl/2017/08/11/why-democrats-should-be-losing-sleep-over-generation-z/#137210b17878.

55 Kate Taylor, "Gen Z Is More Conservative than Many Realize—But the Instagram-Fluent Generation Will Revolutionize the Right," *Business Insider*, accessed September 30, 2020, https://www.businessinsider.com/gen-z-changes-political-divides-2019-7.

I know there are thousands of students with stories just like mine across the nation, and perhaps even the world, who are afraid to speak out. Like those students, I fear that many in my college community may view me differently or look down on me after daring to share the toughest moments of my college experience through this book. However, I fear even *more* that no one will be willing to expose the misguided direction our nation's colleges and universities are barreling toward. I pray that using my voice and sharing my story will inspire other students to do the same by "coming out conservative" on their own campuses.

Despite the leftist insanity that followed me daily, I loved my college experience like any other young adult. I cheered on the home team at football games, ran with the live school mascot on the stadium field, and ate too much pizza in the dining halls. I met new friends and fell in love, studied abroad in beautiful places around the world, received countless opportunities for professional development, challenged myself educationally, and realized my identity as an adult along the way. I will forever be proud to be an alumnus of CSU and will enthusiastically sing the fight song whenever confronting a CU Boulder Buffalo. Out of this love, I share my story, hoping that my university, and many others across the nation, will positively impact young Americans far into the future without succumbing to the failures of leftism, socialism, and extremism.

There are tens of thousands of words in this book, but what I hope this message ultimately boils down to is a single one: **enough**. We've had enough with the leftist indoctrination in our classrooms, with the targeting of conservative student activists for their outspoken values, with the silencing of anything that could remotely become possibly offensive. We're through with failing classes simply because we believe God is real, with administrators pushing a diversity and inclusion agenda, and with being protested simply because we are conservatives. It's time to take our nation's college campuses back. It's time to raise our voices. It's time for universities to offer a true "liberal arts" education—not a "leftist arts" degree. It's time for students to demand more from their college experience as the consumer of education. It's time to expose the true agenda of America's universities and institutions of higher education. It's time for us all, students and alumni alike, to become the "men in the arena" and fight for the future of our colleges and universities and our nation beyond campus.

It's time to fight this culture war on the front lines.

AFTERWORD

As the COVID-19 pandemic has dramatically impacted the student experience on college campuses, I must address the ongoing challenge for the conservative voice at our nation's universities. While classes have largely stopped meeting in person as I finish this manuscript in the winter of 2020, the fight for ideological diversity has become even harder for conservative students.

As a biomedical sciences graduate, something that has shocked me regarding the university response to this pandemic has been the increased push for social justice initiatives during a larger issue—the global pandemic. Students are returning to campus, navigating complex, unprecedented public health guidelines, all while our country responds to the call to action from radical groups like Antifa and Black Lives Matter, Inc. As discussed, universities have responded to these social justice issues in an expected manner—encouraging the Left's perspective while shutting down conservatism—and my alma mater is no exception.

As thousands of new CSU students moved into their dorms

in August 2020, they found themselves present in a quasi-dystopian reality, far from what they imagined as their college experience. Colorful posters of George Floyd and Breonna Taylor's faces lined every dorm hallway, coupled with flyers reading "Black Lives Matter" and "There is no Justice without Racial Justice."

Surely, that would all be shocking enough for a bright-eyed college freshman. But at CSU, freshmen soon received an email from the University President, Joyce McConnell, with the subject line, "COVID Call to Action for CSU Students from President McConnell":

Dear CSU undergraduate, graduate, and professional students,

This is a call to action. You have a responsibility to do what is necessary to mitigate the transmission of the coronavirus at CSU, both on campus and in our community. The vast majority of you are making the right choices; you are responsible, caring, empathetic and willing to take up the challenge and do what is required to stand up against the pandemic. However, some of you are not.

To those of you who are not compliant with state, county and university health protocols: you may be the reason someone loses their life. It is that serious.

[Additional COVID-19-response content removed]

I know that some of you hold political views that you believe justify ignoring state, county, and university public health protocols. Colorado State University respects diverse political views and your freedom to hold them. However, CSU is obligated both legally and morally to do everything we can do—based on the best science available—to establish rules to protect the health of the community and to require you to obey them. We cannot accept your political views as an excuse for non-compliance with state, county, and university rules. This is strictly a public health issue and you will face consequences for non-compliance, including student conduct proceedings and possible expulsion. Don't risk this.

[Additional COVID-19-response content removed]

Sincerely,

Joyce McConnell

President

For a college president to place the burden of responsibility of the spread of a virus on eighteen- and nineteen-year-old students is not just wrong; it's dictatorial. Students are facing extreme campus guidelines, even with mostly online courses, preventing them from being college students in the first place! As thousands of people return to a confined space, a spike in COVID-19 cases is bound to happen, regardless of whether students perfectly follow these "protocols."

I want you to read that email again, specifically the part referencing "political beliefs." This language is dangerous. Very dangerous. It calls out any student of "certain political views" as being dangerous or illegal in their conduct. You can replace the word "certain" with "conservative." The email completely disregards an individual American's First Amendment rights to speech and assembly, despite that this campus is, in fact, located in the United States. If students attend any gathering of more than ten people—on or off campus—they risk expulsion. Current students have informed me that this protocol includes religious services, so this campus, and likely many others, are clearly in violation of the First Amendment's freedom of religion guaranteed to Americans.

Importantly, this rhetoric is dangerous for the mental health of thousands of students. It's hard enough for a young person to stay COVID-free, but the guilt of potentially and unknowingly spreading the virus is more than any person, young or not, should bear. If this is the state of today's universities, then why did they open the campus for students to return in the first place? (What's more, like many schools, CSU *requires* all freshmen to live on campus.)

Simply because campuses look differently than they have in the past does not mean the call to action for conservatives to speak up has changed. In fact, I am of the belief that this call to action matters more today than ever before. The First Amendment is under attack on our college campuses, and it's up to each of us to boldly come out conservative in our collegiate communities to stand up against tyranny.

Moreover, as I write these words, Election Day 2020 has just passed, and the nation awaits final results from the presidential race. In the few weeks since we cast our votes, the radical Left has become even more emboldened in targeting conservatives to silence them.

Recently, the "Million MAGA March" took place in Washington, DC, where voters of President Trump from around the nation marched at our capital city, showing their support for President Trump and the continued election litigation taking place. Hours after the march, as Americans clad in MAGA hats dined in Washington, Antifa and Black Lives Matter, Inc. protesters brutally and violently attacked, throwing punches and explosives to harm those they disagreed with.[56]

Our nation awaits a clear direction under presidential leadership moving forward, but one thing is certain—loud voices in the fight for true unity and liberty are needed today more than ever. No matter who sits in the Oval Office, American citizens must embrace the call to action, to fight in the arena, to lead our culture through truth and courage for ourselves.

Our fight in this culture war has only just begun.

---

56 Michelle Mark, "Violent clashes spark mayhem in DC as counter-protesters brawl with Trump supporters," *Insider*, last modified November 14, 2020, https://www.insider.com/washington-dc-violence-trump-supporters-counterprotesters-brawl-2020-11; Thomas Robertson, "Police arrest DC man in firework attack after Million MAGA March," WTOP News, last modified November 15, 2020, https://wtop.com/dc/2020/11/police-arrest-dc-man-in-firework-attack-after-million-maga-march/.

First day of college at Colorado State University with CAM the Ram

Election Day 2016 on campus

Attending my first Young Women's Leadership Summit with TPUSA, 2017

Working as the Speaker of the Senate with ASCSU

Last day as Speaker of the Senate, 2018

Our TPUSA chapter's first Free Speech Wall on the CSU Plaza, 2017

Free speech walls were our most popular tabling events!

A typical scene tabling for Turning Point USA—lots of discussion and debate!

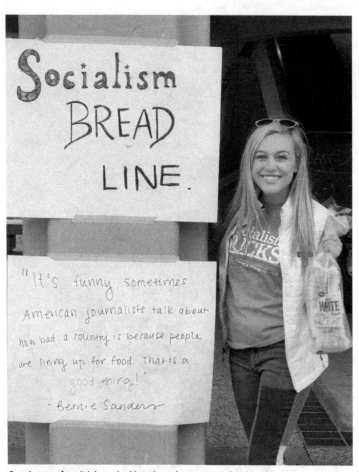

Our chapter often did themed tabling days—here is a socialism bread line.

Getting ready for Charlie Kirk's event at CSU, 2018

Charlie debating CSU students during Q&A, 2018 (Source: Rocky Mountain Collegian)

Student protesters outside of Charlie Kirk event, 2018 (Source: Rocky Mountain Collegian)

Local police prepare for protests at Charlie Kirk event, 2018 (Source: Rocky Mountain Collegian)

Preparing to dismantle protests at Charlie Kirk event, 2018 (Source: Rocky Mountain Collegian)

Antifa clashes with protesters at Charlie Kirk event, 2018 (Source: Rocky Mountain Collegian)

Charlie and Colorado Turning Point USA chapter members, 2018

Candace Owens debates CSU students on the Plaza, 2018 (Source: Rocky Mountain Collegian)

Candace Owens and Colorado Turning Point USA chapter members, 2018

CSU Turning Point members attend CSUnite event, 2018

CSU Students Against White Supremacy at CSUnite event, 2018 (Source: Rocky Mountain Collegian)

CSU Students Against White Supremacy at CSUnite event, 2018 (Source: Rocky Mountain Collegian)

Interning at the White House, summer 2018

Tabling on campus to advertise for Dennis Prager's speech on campus in October 2018

Prepping backstage for Dennis Prager's event at CSU, 2018

Introducing Dennis to the stage, 2018

Dennis Prager addresses the crowd at CSU, 2018

Dennis answers questions from attendees, 2018

The full crowd attending Dennis's speech at CSU—more than 1,200 people!

Colorado State University Turning Point USA Students pose with Dennis Prager following his speech on campus in October 2018

Speaking on behalf of PragerFORCE students at the 2018 PragerU Gala

First time in the PragerU office as a student ambassador, 2018

One of my last tabling events with Turning Point as a student, 2019

Spring in Colorado means senior pictures in the snow! 2019

Graduation day at Colorado State University, 2019

First day filming in the PragerU office, summer 2019

First day filming in the PragerU office, summer 2019

Filming on campus at UC Berkeley with Isabella Chow, the star of the first episode of On The Front Lines, summer 2019

Filming with PragerU at Colorado State University, summer 2019

Cover image of Newsweek Magazine September 2019 issue

Newsweek Magazine MAGA story hits newsstands, fall 2019

First campus speaking event at the University of Nebraska, Lincoln, fall 2019

Filming in the studio with PragerU, winter 2019

Joining the Turning Point USA Contributor Team, February 2020 (graphic courtesy of TPUSA)

ACKNOWLEDGMENTS

Despite feeling isolated on my college campus, my journey is certainly not one of isolation. I have countless people to thank for reminding me of the power of my voice and encouraging me to chase my dream. I would not be here today without their endless and unconditional love and support.

First and foremost, to my team at Scribe Media, especially Jericho—what an amazing experience it has been working with you to turn this book into a reality. Thank you for your endless support and encouragement!

To Mom and Dad—you have always been and likely will always be my biggest cheerleaders. Thank you for forcing me to talk politics with you as a child around the dinner table, making me take notes during every year's State of the Union address, requiring me to join the speech and debate team in high school, and believing I can accomplish anything I set my mind to. You have forever been the perfect example of the American Dream for me, Gaby, and Amelia, and I feel deeply blessed God planned for you to be my parents.

To my sisters, Gaby and Amelia—you've seen my highest of highs and lowest of lows and chosen to love me through it all. They say you can't pick your family, but I would pick you both as my sisters every single time. Thank you for loving me unconditionally, even when I steal clothes from your closets, and for being true examples of Christ's love in my life.

Meemaw & Papa—thank you for consistently demonstrating the reality of the American Dream to me in everything you do. I am inspired by your lives and testimony to the resilience of the American experience. I love you!

To Marcus, Katie, Maggie, and so many family members and friends who have empowered me to use my voice in a big way—I am deeply grateful for your support and encouragement over the past few years, especially as so many others made the decision to end relationships in the face of political differences. God gifted me with such an amazing community in you, and I could not do any of this without your support.

To team PragerU, especially Dennis, Allen, and Marissa—thank you for giving me my first real shot in this industry and for seeing something in me I hadn't even fully seen in myself. I will be eternally grateful for your support and encouragement.

Finally, and importantly, to Charlie, Tyler, and the entire Turning Point USA family—I first fell in love with this movement because of your unique vision for our country and enthusiasm that remains unmatched by any other organization. Thank you for fighting so hard for our great American experiment! *The best is yet to come!*

ABOUT THE AUTHOR

ISABEL BROWN is a Gen Z conservative voice with a bachelor's in biomedical sciences from Colorado State University and a master's in biomedical sciences policy and advocacy from Georgetown. She's a spokesperson for Turning Point USA and the proud host of a TPUSA production, speaking regularly on campuses nationwide.

Isabel is a former U.S. Senate and White House Intern, has produced content with PragerU, and regularly appears on several news networks. You might recognize her from her photo on the cover of *Newsweek* magazine. You can follow Isabel on Instagram/Facebook *@theisabelbrown* and Twitter *@theisabelb*.

CPSIA information can be obtained
at www.ICGtesting.com
Printed in the USA
LVHW051242180723
752689LV00026B/228/J